SKIRTS

SKIRTS

• • •

FASHIONING MODERN FEMININITY IN THE TWENTIETH CENTURY

• • •

KIMBERLY CHRISMAN-CAMPBELL

ST. MARTIN'S PRESS
NEW YORK

First published in the United States by St. Martin's Press,
an imprint of St. Martin's Publishing Group

www.stmartins.com

Designed by Nicola Ferguson

Endpaper art: Reproduction of "A Game of Tennis" Dress Fabric, 1926.
Helen Wills, designer; StehliSilkS Corporation, manufacturer.
Permission to reproduce granted by Allentown Art Museum;
Gift of Kate Fowler Merle-Smith, 1978. (1978.26.165)

Library of Congress Cataloging-in-Publication Data

Names: Chrisman-Campbell, Kimberly, author.
Title: Skirts : fashioning modern femininity in the twentieth century /
    Kimberly Chrisman-Campbell.
Description: First edition. | New York: St. Martin's Press, 2022. |
    Includes bibliographical references and index.
Identifiers: LCCN 2022013245 | ISBN 9781250275790 (hardcover) |
    ISBN 9781250275806 (ebook)
Subjects: LCSH: Skirts—History—20th century. | Femininity—
    In popular culture. | Women—Social conditions—20th century.
Classification: LCC GT2065 .C57 2022 | DDC 391.4/77—dc23/eng
    /20220502
LC record available at https://lccn.loc.gov/2022013245

Our books may be purchased in bulk for promotional, educational,
or business use. Please contact your local bookseller or the Macmillan
Corporate and Premium Sales Department at 1-800-221-7945, extension 5442,
or by email at MacmillanSpecialMarkets@macmillan.com.
First Edition: 2022

10 9 8 7 6 5 4 3 2 1

If I were allowed to choose from the pile of books which will be published one hundred years after my death, do you know which one I would take? No, by no means would I select a novel from that future library—I would simply take a fashion magazine so that I could see how women dress one century after my departure. And these rags would tell me more about the humanity of the future than all the philosophers, novelists, prophets and scholars.

—Anatole France (1844–1924)

CONTENTS

AUTHOR'S NOTE

"Why are you all dressed up?" It's a question I've been hearing my whole life, and the key word is "dress." No one asks a woman why she's all dressed up when she's wearing jeans, or even a sleek, sharp pantsuit. But put on a skirt—any skirt—and suddenly you're being fancy.

Skirts have long been an obsession of mine, both personally and professionally. My first published article was about the mother of all skirts, the eighteenth-century hoop petticoat. In it, I discussed the primal appeal of enormous skirts, which emphasized (or at least gave the illusion of) a narrow waist and wide hips, telegraphing both virginity and fertility, two qualities that have historically been universally valued in women. That psychosexual subtext is likely lost on the millions of little girls who dream of dressing like Disney princesses, or the jaded fashion editors who stayed behind after Christian Dior's debut fashion show to twirl around in his decadently long New Look skirts. But it's there nonetheless. When you study historic fashion for a living, wearing long, full, multilayered skirts seems not just normal but sensible, and I increasingly practiced what I preached. Longtime friends who have never, ever seen me in pants laughed when I told them I was writing a book about skirts, dubbing it my "anti-pants manifesto."

I was born in 1973, the same year as Diane von Furstenberg's wrap dress. Pants were finally becoming part of mainstream women's fashion in a serious way, but designers like von Furstenberg were pushing back, arguing (very successfully) that skirts still had their place. My relationship with pants might be different today had I been born a decade or two earlier—or later—and it's unlikely that I would associate wearing a skirt with "dressing up" rather than "getting dressed." My first fashion role model was Audrey Hepburn as Holly Golightly in *Breakfast at Tiffany's,* who seemed to wear chic black evening gowns 24/7. Whatever her job was, I wanted it. I was too young to understand the circa-1960 call-girl lifestyle; to me, it was a fashion choice.

But it never occurred to me to stop wearing pants altogether; indeed, as a child of the 1970s, I remember too well wearing dresses *over* pants. Growing up, I was suspicious of my female classmates who only wore skirts—generally frilly floral frocks and ruffled skirts by Laura Ashley or Gunne Sax. They were the same girls who took ballet lessons and collected ringleted dolls and threw princess-themed birthday parties and cosplayed *Little House on the Prairie,* and I wanted nothing to do with their performative femininity. Instead, I practiced what then passed for performative feminism: I may have idolized Audrey Hepburn, but I also loved sporty Esprit separates, Barbies, *Charlie's Angels,* Lynda Carter's Wonder Woman, and skirted sleuth Nancy Drew. When I moved from sunny California to drizzly England for graduate school, I was as likely to wear pants as long, wooly skirts—anything to keep from freezing to death. (I also learned to call them "trousers"; in British English, "pants" denotes "underpants.")

It wasn't until I finished grad school and got a job in the museum field that I virtually banished pants from my wardrobe. Working in a Gilded Age historic house encouraged a certain degree of formality, and you never knew when you were going to run into an elderly donor or trustee with conservative ideas about appropriate office attire. My female bosses wore not just skirts but pantyhose and heels every single day; some looked like chic corporate lawyers, others perpetually dressed like the mother of the bride in floaty pastels and pearls. I was not entirely surprised to learn in the course of researching this book that another historic house museum, The Frick Collection, required some of its female *visitors* to wear skirts well into the 1980s.

As a textile lover, I've always been happiest wearing as much fabric as physically possible, and, as a historian, I appreciated the rich heritage of skirts and their role in female self-fashioning. As an impecunious newbie curator, throwing on a dress was the easiest and most economical way to look both professional and pulled together; all I had to do was add shoes and maybe a piece of vintage-store statement jewelry. Over time, my starving-student figure settled into a curvier silhouette, and skirts were undeniably more flattering than the low-rise and "skinny" trouser styles then in fashion. At some point, I realized that I need never again worry about how my butt looked in pants, or whether a waistband would dig in or stretch out over the course of the day, or how to keep my trouser socks from slouching down. My sex had gone hundreds of years without wearing pants. I could, too.

I wasn't alone. The early twenty-first century saw a dress renaissance led by a new generation of women in power, with an assist from *Mad Men*, the midcentury-set television drama that premiered in 2007, inspiring a trend for vintage and vintage-inspired fashion. Suddenly, even mall stores were full of dresses with swishy skirts, generous hemlines, and capacious pockets—something jeggings just couldn't offer. A woman didn't have to wear a suit to be taken seriously in the workplace, or on the world stage. Thanks to the revival of the midi length, there was no danger of bending over or getting caught in a breeze and exposing an eyeful of thigh. Around the same time, many straight-size brands began offering tall and petite sizes, meaning hemlines were never too high or too low. "I don't love pants," actress Reese Witherspoon confessed to the *Los Angeles Times* when she launched her Southern-accented fashion label Draper James in October 2015. "To be totally honest they're not my thing, probably because I'm five-two and they make me look really short. I like wearing dresses because they're easy, and I like skirts." The "one and done" aspect of the dress is central to its appeal to modern women: while the dress may seem fussy or formal to those who associate it with the nostalgic femininity of weddings, proms, and quinceañeras, it can also be functional and efficient—the essence of modernity.

Today, I have one pair of "emergency jeans" that I keep for those rare occasions when I feel like hiking or gardening, and some yoga pants that I never, ever wear outside of the gym. (As the late Karl Lagerfeld said, "sweatpants are a sign of defeat.") But the rest of my wardrobe consists of skirts and dresses, most of them knee-length or longer. And the truth is, there's not much I want to do that I can't do in a skirt. I even have a modern version of Claire McCardell's Pop-Over, a sturdy denim wrap dress that's ideal for doing housework. I wrote this entire book while wearing dresses around the house *during a global pandemic*. Take that, Holly Golightly.

But *Skirts* really isn't an anti-pants manifesto. I wholeheartedly agree with *Vogue*'s 1964 stance that pants are a great thing "on the proper figure" and "on the proper occasion." If I had a different body or lifestyle, I'd wear them more often. But I believe there will always be a place for skirts in women's wardrobes, and their history has much to teach us about the changing expression and definition of femininity (and masculinity) over the course of the twentieth century. This book is intended to correct some outdated and even damaging misconceptions about dresses. The same kinds of misconceptions have tended to follow other women's garments like corsets and high heels—both of which have enjoyed unnaturally long life spans despite changing fashions and harsh criticism from men, for the simple reason that women actually like them, or at least reap benefits that outweigh the inconveniences of wearing them. Pants aren't likely to go away, but they were never intended to replace skirts, and I hope they never will.

ACKNOWLEDGMENTS

This project was the brainchild of Stephen Power at St. Martin's Press, and I am grateful to Sarah Grill for shepherding it to completion with enthusiasm and insight, as well as to copy editor Laura Dragonette, and my always-stylish agent, Laurie Fox. *The Atlantic* kindly allowed me to reprint portions of my articles "*Cinderella:* The Ultimate (Postwar) Makeover Story," "The Midi Skirt, Divider of Nations," "Wimbledon's First Fashion Scandal," and "When American Suffragists Tried to 'Wear the Pants.'" I am also indebted to *Ornament,* where I first wrote about Mary Quant. Many scholars, curators, and archivists helped me gather the information and images within. I am especially grateful to Susan North and Alden O'Brien. I thank my family—Ian, Rory, and Ramsay—for their encouragement and support as I worked on this **dream project** under less-than-dreamy circumstances. *Skirts* is dedicated to my friend and mentor Aileen Ribeiro, who taught me everything I know about historical dress, then turned around and pushed me to engage with contemporary fashion. As usual, she was right.

SKIRTS

INTRODUCTION

"Feel like a woman, wear a dress!" the ads read. In 1973, as women were entering the workforce in record numbers, and increasingly "wearing the pants" both literally and metaphorically, Diane von Furstenberg made a compelling case for the dress as a practical, modern, and feminist fashion statement. Buyers responded, and her instantly iconic wrap dresses went on sale to the public in April 1974. By 1975, von Furstenberg was selling 15,000 of them per week, though the inevitable knockoffs and market saturation meant that the demand dried up by 1978. In 1997, however, von Furstenberg reintroduced the apparently timeless style to a ravenous market; the company reaped $500 million in revenue in 2015, more than forty years after the wrap dress was first launched.

Dresses have long been synonymous with femininity in Western culture. (In Eastern history, the story of skirts—and pants—as expressions of gender identity is more nuanced. By the twentieth century, however, the dictates of Paris couturiers were understood and heeded around the world.) One of the earliest and most enduring forms of clothing, worn from about 20,000 BC through the Bronze Age, was a fringed apron known as a string skirt, which likely advertised a woman's childbearing abilities.[1] "The skirt is a feminine symbol," designer and skirt aficionado Miuccia Prada told *The New York Times* in 2006. She later explained: "To me, the waist up is more spiritual, more intellectual, while the waist down is more basic, more grounded. It's about sex. It's about making love. It's about life. It's about giving birth. Basically, below the waist is more connected to the earth."[2] The skirt's pyramidal form has become visual shorthand for the female body itself. Want to feminize your restroom sign or anthropomorphic cartoon character? Put a skirt on it!

As well as sexual identity, skirts communicate social standing; historically, long, full skirts have served as canvases for expensive textiles and trimmings. During the Renaissance, for example, Venetian women wore tall platform shoes called chopines in order to bypass sumptuary laws restricting the use of luxury textiles; the high heels necessitated extra inches of fabric. Many such seemingly irrational fashions—not just chopines but farthingales, hoops, crinolines, and bustles—make sense when viewed through the lens of conspicuous consumption. Long, cumbersome skirts also advertised that a woman didn't need to work (or walk anywhere) and ensured that both her body and behavior conformed to unassailable standards of modesty. To the skirt's sexual and economic implications were added the haptic pleasures of skirt wearing, from the sensual swishing and swirling of a full skirt to the satisfying constraint of a pencil skirt, a hobble skirt, or a bodycon dress.

Beginning in the late Middle Ages, when men stopped wearing long robes, "revealing the legs was a symbol of masculinity" and "a mark of phallic power," while covering them signified feminine modesty.[3] Critiques of women's fashions have often

served as thinly veiled attacks on women—targeting their perceived frivolity, vanity, or sexual immorality—but women and
their clothes have been linked in a more literal sense, as well.
It was in the 1500s—shortly after men gave up long robes for
short doublets and hose—that "skirts" first became slang for
women themselves. Historically, it has been a pejorative term.
A womanizer was a "skirt chaser"; a "light skirt" might allow
herself to be caught. The etymology is both older and younger
than it seems; the *Oxford English Dictionary* documents the use
of "skirt" as a metonym for "woman" as early as 1578, while
the Beastie Boys celebrated "skirt chasing" in their 1986 rap
"Rhymin & Stealin." As the language of fashion changed, so did
the idioms it inspired. By the nineteenth century, women in positions of power were belittled as "petticoat government"—or,
alternatively, accused of "wearing the pants." In *As You Like It*
(1599), Shakespeare's heroine Rosalind (masquerading as a man)
feels compelled to "comfort the weaker vessel, as doublet and
hose ought to show itself courageous to petticoat"; the funnel-
shaped petticoat (a synonym for "skirt" at the time) is linguisti-
cally upended to represent an inferior "vessel."

Three centuries later, women were still being defined by their
dresses. Another romantic comedy, the 1952 musical film *Skirts
Ahoy!*—a Korean War sequel of sorts to 1945's *Anchors Aweigh*—
followed the amorous adventures of three Navy WAVES (an
acronym denoting Women Accepted for Volunteer Emergency
Service). The characters wore skirt suits based on the much-
praised real-life uniforms designed by Chicago-born couturier Mainbocher for the women's service branch in 1942 (see
Plate 1). (Though female volunteers were sorely needed to
allow more men to fight overseas, the idea of putting women

in uniform remained controversial, and the last thing anyone wanted to do was invite comparisons to their male counterparts by dressing them in pants.) The film combined you-go-girl navy recruitment propaganda with retrograde songs like "What Good Is a Gal (Without a Guy)." The trailer touted: "Sailors who go down to the sea in . . . slips!"

The difference between "dresses" and "skirts" was largely semantic until the mid-twentieth century. Not all skirts are dresses, though all dresses have skirts. But women have always worn the two interchangeably, a practice reflected in the imprecise terminology used to describe them; many of the "dresses" and "gowns" of the seventeenth, eighteenth, and nineteenth centuries actually consisted of two pieces, if not three or four. The shirtwaist—a menswear-inspired blouse, worn with a long skirt—was a daywear staple at the beginning of the twentieth century; however, it was the noteworthy top that gave the ensemble its name. The concept of "separates"—mix and match jackets, sweaters, blouses, skirts, and occasionally even culottes or "slacks"—only emerged in the 1930s, as women began to lead more active lifestyles and travel frequently, requiring versatile capsule wardrobes. World War II fabric shortages made separates an economical and patriotic choice; re-wearing a handful of pieces in different combinations meant that a woman needed fewer of them. In 1942, *Vogue* devoted several pages to the then-novel concept: "We expect clothes to be good-looking and . . . able to do double, triple, quadruple duty . . . expectations that are all fulfilled by separate skirts." Once again, skirts stood in for women themselves, who were expected to do their "duty" to their country by looking good and embracing the make-do-and-mend ethos.

The story of women's liberation—political and sartorial—is often framed by the growing acceptance of pants over the twentieth century. Early, abortive attempts by Victorian feminists and dress reformers to popularize pants proved to be unhelpful distractions from their causes. Even suffragist Amelia Bloomer, for whom the bifurcated bloomer costume was named, gave it up after a few years. "We were not willing to sacrifice greater questions to it," she admitted.

From failed experiments with bloomers in the 1850s to the cycling craze of the 1890s; from Coco Chanel's "beach pyjamas" of the 1920s to Rosie the Riveter's coveralls; from Yves Saint Laurent's "Le Smoking" pantsuit of 1966 to the pantsuit First Lady (and Senate candidate) Hillary Clinton wore at the 2000 Democratic National Convention, pants have been a symbolic and sometimes physical expression of the new, less tangible freedoms that opened to women. As Bloomer herself pointed out, adopting

FIGURE 1. Amelia Bloomer, "originator of the new dress," appeared in *The Illustrated London News* wearing her innovative hybrid costume, but soon gave it up, calling it an unhelpful distraction from "greater questions." (*The Illustrated London News, September 27, 1851*)

traditionally male garments was tantamount to an across-the-board "usurpation of the rights of man"—whether the right to vote or the right to run for president. By the 1840s, "wearing the pants" (or "trousers," in Britain) was a colloquialism for holding the dominant position in a male–female relationship—one that could exist only because pants were understood to be an exclusively male garment. This was not to suggest that pants were synonymous with power, or a proxy for it, but that power (like pants) properly belonged to men alone.

It's an inconvenient truth that women kept on wearing dresses even as pants became increasingly available to them, whether by choice or because the social and physical "freedoms" pants purportedly offered were largely illusive. Even voluminous or wide-legged pants designed for riding, bicycling, or hiking could be quickly converted into skirts by means of button flaps, ensuring modesty and propriety. Women who did wear pants were not necessarily laborers in need of practical workwear; often, they were privileged elites who deliberately challenged gender norms for a provocatively feminist or erotically androgynous effect, like Marlene Dietrich, Greta Garbo, or Katharine Hepburn. (Hepburn was not actually opposed to skirts but hated wearing the stockings and garter belts that inevitably accompanied them before the advent of pantyhose and tights in the 1960s; many of the perennial critiques of skirts have been predicated on accessories like petticoats, girdles, pantyhose, or high heels.) Pants remained on the fringes of women's fashion for much of the twentieth century; they weren't permitted in many offices, nightclubs, country clubs, churches, classrooms, or restaurants until the 1970s. Even in freezing climates, school dress codes often required female students to wear skirts, and frequently specified a conservative length, neither long "granny dresses" nor miniskirts. Mary Tyler Moore was a capri pants–wearing pioneer on *The Dick Van Dyke Show,* the sitcom that premiered in 1961. But her character, Laura Petrie, was a suburban housewife, and initially the actress was allowed to wear pants in only one scene per episode. When, in 1970, Moore played an unmarried big-city career woman in her eponymous television show, she sported office-appropriate skirts.

Wearing pants was frequently treated as a literal crime of fashion; in the nineteenth century, women in bloomers and other bifurcated garments risked being arrested under laws banning cross-dressing. Many were suffragists and dress reformers who deliberately courted controversy, but the arrests continued even as pants began to creep into mainstream women's fashion. In 1933, Joanne Cummings was arrested for wearing pants in public in New York. In 1938, Los Angeles kindergarten teacher Helen Hulick was barred from testifying in a burglary case (three times!) when she arrived at the courthouse wearing trousers. The city of Florence, Italy, levied fines on women wearing pants and shorts in 1941; if they were caught while riding a bicycle, the bicycle was confiscated. Evelyn Bross was charged for wearing trousers on a Chicago street in 1943, even though she was dressed for her job as a machinist in a war plant. She was acquitted; as the judge explained, "I think the fact that girls wear slacks should not be held against them when they are not deliberately impersonating men. Styles are changing."[4] (While the term "slacks"—originally meaning loosely fitting trousers—is usually associated with women's pants, it was used for menswear much earlier, in the 1820s.) In separate, well-publicized incidents in the 1980s, female lawyers in Canada, Australia, and Puerto Rico were banned from courtrooms by male judges for wearing pants—bans they successfully sued to overturn.

Yet these aren't just quaint history lessons; legal disputes over appropriately gendered attire are more timely than ever, and pants are still banned today in many countries and contexts. In 2009, journalist Lubna Hussein went to jail for wearing wide-legged pants in violation of Sudan's Islamic indecency laws; she was one of 43,000 women arrested in Khartoum in a single year for clothing-related offenses, many of them from predominantly Christian southern Sudan. Religious prejudices against pants persist in the United States, too, and they are often tied up with broader controversies over sexual identity and gender nonconformity. As recently as 2016, a lesbian student in Harrisburg, Pennsylvania, was refused admission to her Catholic high school's prom for wearing a tuxedo; a school official threatened to call the police.[5]

As wide-legged culottes, skorts, and gauchos appeared on runways and retail racks in the 1970s, many women and girls tried to skirt the skirt rules, only to be turned away by doormen, maître d's, principals, and other (male) gatekeepers who equated divided skirts with pants. Until 1989, The Frick Collection, a museum in industrialist Henry Clay Frick's former Fifth Avenue home, kept a loaner wrap skirt in the cloakroom of its Art Reference Library for female researchers who turned up in pants—a rule instituted by founder Helen Clay Frick. (Men had to wear jackets.) Some of the more conservative New York law firms didn't permit their female employees to wear pants until the early 1990s; pants were tacitly banned from the floor of the United States Senate until 1993. In a 1995 *New Yorker* cartoon, a secretary announces to her boss: "A couple of suits and a skirt to see you." Not only were women still slangily defined by their skirts, but the metonym had metastasized to menswear. A French law against women wearing pants, which was passed in 1800 in the wake of the social and sartorial upheavals of the French Revolution, wasn't formally overturned until 2013—though freedom of dress was one of the Revolution's most cherished tenets. British Airways flight attendants had to wait until 2016. Even when these institutions grudgingly permitted "slacks," jeans and shorts often remained firmly forbidden. When Minnie Mouse celebrated International Women's Day 2022 and the thirtieth anniversary of Disneyland Paris by swapping her red dress for a Stella McCartney pantsuit, Fox News pundit Candace Owens criticized Disney for "making her more masculine" in an attempt to "destroy fabrics of our society."

When women did dare to wear pants, they puzzled over what to wear under them. In June 1943, as women entered the war effort and donned jeans and coveralls, a *Vogue* piece recommended flesh-colored rayon jersey underpants with "a nude, nonexistent look," explaining that "no other lingerie is so bulkless under blue jeans. So right for slacks and shorts. For climbing to the tip of a giant airplane-in-the-making." The article linked the new barely-there, wash-and-wear rayon bras, slips, and panties to modernity, in both the technological and ideological senses: "Simplification is a twentieth-century word." But conquering visible panty lines, or "VPL" (a term popularized by the famously pants-forward 1977 film *Annie Hall*), proved to be anything but simple. Panty-line-preventing thongs inspired another damning phrase, "whale tail," coined in the late 1990s to describe the part of a thong visible above the rear waistband of a woman's low-rise pants, which resembled the flukes of the marine mammal; Monica Lewinsky famously flashed hers at President Bill Clinton in 1995.

The checkered history of pants for women is inscribed in their construction and production. Many of the early female adopters of pants were wealthy women who enjoyed riding and other country pursuits in pants custom-made by their husbands' tailors, ensuring a flattering and comfortable fit. Katharine Hepburn had hers made by Spencer Tracy's Beverly Hills tailor Eddie Schmidt, or Savile Row's H. Huntsman & Sons, who dressed her frequent costar Cary Grant. Even now, mass-produced men's pants are available in a vastly wider range of sizes, accounting for both waist and inseam measurements; the standard size range might offer seventy-two distinct options, without including big and tall or short sizes. By contrast, women's pants sizes follow the same limited numerical system as dresses and other types of womenswear. Only women's jeans are sized by waist and inseam like men's pants, though this precision is not always helpful, as women's bodies tend to have wider discrepancies between their waist and hip measurements. Levi's began offering a made-to-measure jeans service in 1994, followed by Lands' End in 2001. Not Your Daughter's Jeans—the California label founded in 2003, amid the low-rise denim trend—distinguished itself by offering off-the-rack women's jeans in an unprecedented sixty-six sizes, including petite, plus, tall, and short options.

Not surprisingly, given their sizing issues, one of the perennial complaints against women wearing pants was that they were unflattering. A 1939 *Vogue* article headlined "Slacks and Skirts for Country Living" condescendingly advised: "You'll want—if you weigh under a hundred and fifty—a pair or two of slacks. . . . Not necessarily tailored like a man's—after all, your figure isn't the same. . . . If you have hips, try wearing that long cardigan . . . or, for dinner, a flaring tunic." (Contrarian fashion designer Elizabeth Hawes countered: "There are just as many men with round hips and protruding tummies as there are ladies.") The article specified that pants should only be worn "on your own property . . . on the beach . . . on small boats. . . . On ocean liners, they're usually restricted to the sports deck." In July 1964, as pants were beginning to creep from country and resort wardrobes into city life, *Vogue* once again offered highly conditional praise: "On the proper figure—slim-hipped, really narrow through the thighs—on the proper occasion, pants are a sharp, smart turnout, completely correct for our time. . . . Pants are indeed for the private life." At the time, many designers only offered pants in women's sizes up to 12 (size 6 or 8 in modern sizing), suggesting that they were proper not just for the private life but for only the very petite. If women have continued to choose dresses, it is partly because they are more forgiving to the female figure than mass-produced pants and thus more comfortable, both physically and psychologically.

Without suggesting that the much-vaunted fashion gains women made over the twentieth century were trivial or merely symbolic, I want to propose an alternative interpretation: namely, that skirts are not necessarily opposite or inferior to pants in terms of comfort, novelty, utility, modernity, or progressivism. Certainly, women have long managed to climb

FIGURE 2. Lucy Smith, cofounder of the Ladies Scottish Climbing Club, and Pauline Ranken scale Salisbury Crags in Edinburgh in June 1908. (*Courtesy Ladies Scottish Climbing Club*)

mountains, explore jungles, ride horses and bicycles, perform manual labor, and enjoy sports like gymnastics, fencing, skiing, and even boxing while wearing skirts, if only because they had no other option.

It has become a lazy cliché of costume drama—the "fake history of costume," as fashion historian Anne Hollander called it in her book *Seeing Through Clothes*—to put a heroine in pants or breeches in order to signal that she is sporty, adventurous, rebellious, or somehow "not like other girls." Certainly, some daring female celebrities like Bloomer, Dietrich, Hepburn, and Amelia Earhart became doubly famous for embracing pants. But suffragists and soldiers marched in skirts. The heroines of the civil rights movement—Rosa Parks, Ruby Bridges, two-thirds of the Little Rock Nine, and the Bloody Sunday marchers in their church clothes—took a stand in skirts. Frida Kahlo and Georgia O'Keeffe revolutionized modern art in skirts. Marie Curie won two Nobel Prizes in a skirt. When NASA put a man on the moon, "the computer wore a skirt," in the words of one of those computers, mathematician Katherine G. Johnson.

Even as they were increasingly given the option of wearing pants—an ostensibly more practical and comfortable alternative—women continued to wear skirts, this time by choice. Shirley Chisholm, who in 1968 became the first Black woman elected to Congress and ran for president in 1972, was known for her boldly patterned dresses and skirt suits, many of which she designed herself. Once, her staff persuaded her to wear a pantsuit in the House of Representatives, as some other female legislators had begun to do. Even though she hid it under an ankle-length sleeveless coat, her press aide recalled: "She was so embarrassed, she kept her head in her newspapers. She

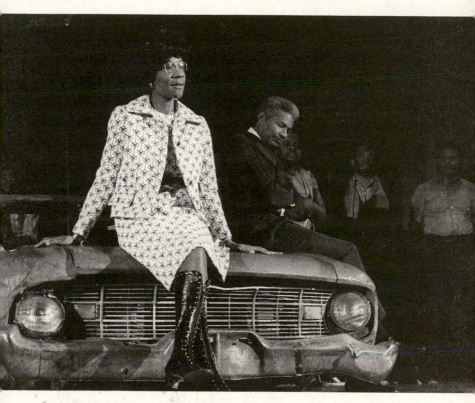

FIGURE 3. U.S. Representative Shirley Chisholm—the first Black woman elected to Congress—discusses her upcoming presidential run with a New York theater audience in 1972. (*AP / Shutterstock.com*)

must have read *The New York Times* seven times that day." For a woman who was never shy about jumping into a debate, it was an uncharacteristic posture. While Chisholm wore pants and culottes in private, when it came to her professional life, she was more comfortable in a skirt.

Today, women have a much wider arsenal of fashion expression available to them—certainly wider than men, who, for all their power and privilege, have only recently branched out into dresses and skirts (as opposed to kilts, kaftans, sarongs, dhotis, and other traditional skirted garments coded as masculine or unisex). Just as Amelia Bloomer and her fellow suffragists realized that pants were hurting rather than helping their cause, so women of the twentieth century found that they did not need to "wear the pants" to wield power and influence, or to dress in a way that was both practical and progressive. As women made strides toward social as well as physical freedom—winning the right to vote and to participate in the military, the government, and the workforce—their wardrobes evolved with them. Rather than embodying an outdated stereotype of femininity, the dress itself became modern. Designers like Mariano Fortuny, Chanel, and Jean Patou redefined the dress for the twentieth century, taking inspiration from history while embracing new tastes and technologies. Hemlines climbed higher, and silhouettes grew more body-conscious. Stripped of constraining undergarments like corsets and crinolines, the dress reemerged in the twentieth century as both timeless and entirely modern. Indeed, the most important and influential female fashions of the era were skirted, while pants for women remained marginalized and controversial until the mid-1970s.

Skirts looks at the history of twentieth-century womenswear through the lens of these game-changing garments, including famous styles like the little black dress and the Bar Suit as well as more obscure innovations like the Pop-Over dress—which came with a matching pot holder—and the Taxi dress, an ancestor of von Furstenberg's wrap dress. It examines the roles of the media, the internet, and celebrities in publicizing and popularizing new fashions and considers the contributions of major designers such as Yves Saint Laurent, Halston, Issey

Miyake, Alexander McQueen, and Donatella Versace. While all of the styles featured in the book originated in the twentieth century, their influence continues to shape contemporary fashion today. These innovative, influential garments illuminate the unique times in which they were first worn and the women who wore them, but they also have lasting fashion legacies and continue to be reinterpreted by designers decades later. The story of skirts in the twentieth century charts the changing fortunes, freedoms, and aspirations of women themselves.

1

THE DELPHOS

Goddess Dressing

The dawn of a new year—or a new century—is a time for retrospection as much as anticipation, reevaluating what worked and what didn't, what's destined for the dustbin of history and what's worth hanging on to. In the first decade of the twentieth century, fashion looked backward: beyond the sprung-steel crinolines and steam-molded corsets born of the Industrial Revolution, beyond the oppressive luxuries of the ancien régime, to the vanishingly distant past. Thanks to new technologies—the mechanical cotton gin, the power loom, the sewing machine, the metal grommet—female dress had become mired in ornament over the course of the nineteenth century, the female body pinched and padded beyond recognition, twisted into unnatural curves, and topped with hats so large, so laden with feathers that women looked like "decorated bundles," in fashion designer Paul Poiret's phrase.[1] In order to move forward, fashion had to go back—all the way to the beginning.

In ancient times, those seeking guidance consulted an oracle. The most famous oracle inhabited the Temple of Apollo at Delphi, the Grecian city named for Apollo's son Delphos. It was to Delphi that fashion designer Mariano Fortuny looked for inspiration—specifically the Hellenistic bronze sculpture of the Charioteer of Delphi, rediscovered in an unusually good state of preservation by French archaeologists in 1896, the same year that the first modern Olympic Games took place in Athens. The life-sized statue is clothed in a long, pleated tunic called a chiton, belted above the waist, with thin straps crossing its back and shoulders; the garment's lines emphasize the youthful figure's tall, slim build. It is as unexpected as it is striking, for Greek athletes competed in the nude; the sculptor probably intended to depict a victory lap rather than a moment in the chariot race.

Instead of being tailored according to the complex clothing architecture perfected over the course of the early modern period, ancient garments often consisted of uncut cloth taken straight off the loom, which was draped and pinned or tied in place, with minimal stitching. Yet they can be deceptive in their apparent simplicity. In ancient Egypt, linen garments were pleated horizontally, using a method that has never been discovered but was so effective that surviving examples retain those pleats to this day. The Roman toga had to be precisely woven to a semicircular shape in order to drape correctly, as anyone who tries to re-create the look with a rectangular bedsheet quickly learns.

The Greeks, however, created clothing out of carefully folded and pinned rectangles of fabric, and Fortuny did the same. The three main garments worn by men and women alike in ancient Greece were the himation, a shawl or mantle; the chiton, a rectangle folded in half then fastened along the upper arms to create sleeves; and the peplos, a square folded in half then pinned at each shoulder and belted and folded over at the waist. Fortuny's Delphos gown of 1909 was constructed of four or five pieces of pleated fabric hand-sewn into a tube, gathered at the neck, and fastened at intervals by beads interlaced with cording along the upper arm (the ancient version used decorative pins called fibulae).

Instead of translucent linen, he used imported Japanese silk, hand-dyed in rich monochromatic hues and pleated using a time-consuming, patented process involving heated porcelain tubes that has never been successfully replicated. Albumin, made from egg whites, was brushed on to fix the pleats while enhancing the silk's brilliance and softness. "Sheer Tanagra loveliness," *Vogue* pronounced the Delphos, invoking the terra-cotta figurines first produced in Greece in the fourth century BC. The dress tapped into a time-honored ideal of beauty, turning mortal women into goddesses and infusing an ephemeral garment with the weight of thousands of years of history.

A variant of the Delphos, the Peplos had a waist-length overtunic attached along the neckline to a sleeveless underdress. The hem of the tunic approximated the apoptygma, or overfold, at the waist that was a feature of the classical peplos. It was longer at the sides, a structural detail of a true peplos that Fortuny recreated for decorative effect. The pleats and gathers of the gowns echoed the fluting of ancient architectural columns. But they were not just decorative elements. The pleats lent the fabric an elastic quality; unlike Poiret's notorious hobble skirt, the Delphos achieved its cylindrical silhouette without impeding

FIGURE 4. Dancer Isadora Duncan's daughters Margot, Anna, and Lisa in Fortuny gowns, c. 1920. (*Museum of Performance & Design*)

movement. In the absence of seaming or understructure, the pleats also gave the dress its shape—or, rather, they ensured that the dress conformed to the contours of the wearer's body, moving, expanding, and contracting with it. "They clung like a mermaid's scales," remembered Fortuny's client Lady Diana Cooper.[2] As curator Harold Koda has pointed out, "this celebration of the natural female form, together with the idea of apparel based on simple geometries manipulated into diverse effects, made the dress of the ancient Greeks an apt paradigm for twentieth-century designers who were engaged by the strategies of modernism."[3] The dresses were long enough to pool around the wearer's feet, a detail borrowed from ancient vase paintings. Murano glass beads strung on silk cords and applied around the hemlines were not only eye-catching but functional, weighing down the silk and ensuring that it fell smoothly. The dresses could be worn on their own or paired with one of Fortuny's long "Knossos" scarves or coats and tunics block-printed and stenciled with motifs from Cycladic art.

Fortuny was a scientist as much as an artist. Born amid the Islamic splendor of Granada, he moved to the equally storied and opulent city of Venice at the age of twenty. He spent the rest of his life there, at the crossroads of Orient and Occident, opening his design house in 1906. Surrounded by Byzantine luxury, and working in isolation, far from the strictly regimented ateliers of Parisian haute couture, he developed a unique sartorial vocabulary and pioneered innovative techniques for dyeing and weaving, printing and pleating cloth. He received more than twenty patents for his inventions—though he noted in the margin of his patent application for the Delphos that he shared the credit with his wife, Henriette.

Fortuny was hardly the first designer to take inspiration from classical antiquity. The neoclassical revival of the late eighteenth century—which touched furniture, art, and architecture as well as fashion—was, like the Delphos, inspired by archaeology: excavations of the ancient cities of Pompeii and Herculaneum began in the mid-eighteenth century, exciting widespread interest in ancient art and culture. Marie-Antoinette and other ladies of the French court adopted simple white muslin gowns imitating unearthed marble statuary, even if that marble was originally painted in vibrant colors. Lady Emma Hamilton, the wife of the British ambassador to Naples, became known for her "attitudes," a form of performance art inspired by her husband's collection of ancient statues and vases. Scantily clad in diaphanous robes and shawls, she entertained friends and visitors by striking a series of dramatic poses inspired by classical art. Melesina St. George recorded in her diary: "She disposes the shawls so as to form Grecian, Turkish, and other drapery, as well as a variety of turbans. Her arrangement of the turbans is absolute sleight of hand, she does it so quickly, so easily, and so well."

The "Empire line" of the early nineteenth century was actually the high, belted waist of ancient Greece; ladies of Napoleon's court wore it with jewelry and hairstyles "à l'antique" copied from busts of Roman empresses. "Etruscan" motifs or designs "à la Grec" replaced the undulating ribbons, flowers, and feathers of the ancien régime; cameos and gold armbands replaced diamonds and pearls. While Marie-Antoinette had kept her arms and ankles covered, the French Revolution introduced relaxed sexual mores along with radical political reforms. Thin white muslin sheaths with high waistlines and

low necklines mimicked the clinging drapery of classical statues, baring the upper arms and outlining the legs for the first
time in centuries. The Duchesse d'Abrantès complained: "No
way to cheat nature anymore. These days a plain woman tends
to look even plainer, and a woman with a bad figure is lost. It
is only the slender ones with a mass of hair and a small bosom
who triumph."[4] The emperor's wife, Joséphine Bonaparte, was
among the lucky few.

Imaginative accessories completed the Hellenic tableau.
High-heeled shoes were replaced by flat cothurnes; these lightweight sandals laced up the leg, calling attention to bare flesh
or flesh-colored stockings. Cashmere shawls mimicked the
drapery of antique statues and provided much-needed warmth;
the traditional teardrop-shaped pine cone pattern and discreet
floral motifs added visual interest to plain white gowns. These
shawls first appeared in French fashion magazines and por-
traits in 1790, although they did not become widely available
until Napoleon's campaigns in Egypt, where Indian shawls
were easily obtained from traders.

With Napoleon's exile to Elba and the restoration of the
French monarchy, fashion became more conservative and covered up. In England, Queen Victoria promoted middle-class
morality and modeled sober respectability. The mechanization
of weaving and sewing made fashionable clothing more affordable and elaborately decorative; chemical dyes made it more
colorful, to the point that some found it unsightly. Steel boning
and metal eyelets enabled the construction of ever more disfiguring corsets, crinolines, and bustles. Dress reform activists
attacked these ornate garments and complex understructures
as both ugly and unhealthy; they proposed more attractive and

"hygienic" alternatives like warm woolen underwear, divided skirts, petticoats weighing less than seven pounds, and clothes inspired by the dress of the preindustrial past. Many artists— including leaders of the Pre-Raphaelite Brotherhood of painters, founded in England in 1848, and the English Arts and Crafts Movement—also revolted against modern dress, using models wearing carefully researched and re-created classical and medieval dress and hairstyles, without modern underpinnings, to depict historical and mythological subjects.

Fortuny, too, sought to banish unnatural underpinnings and introduce "rational" and "aesthetic" fashions. His dresses may have been inspired by antiquity, but they were entirely modern in their innovative construction techniques and body-conscious silhouettes. "Gone were the buttoned boots, the curves, the boned collars, the straight-fronted stays," Lady Cooper exulted. "Greek—everything must be Greek. I must . . . have a crescent in my hair, draperies, sandaled or bare feet, . . . peplums, . . . shining white limbs."[5] Though too daring (and too expensive) for the masses, they were embraced by aristocrats like Cooper and high-profile actresses and artists—women with enough money, audacity, or social clout to spurn convention. The Marchesa Luisa Casati was one of Fortuny's first customers. Modern dance pioneers Isadora Duncan, Ruth St. Denis, and Loïe Fuller performed their avant-garde dances in Delphos gowns, channeling the gyrations and bare limbs of the Bacchantes and Minoan women who had inspired Fortuny's creations. The actresses Sarah Bernhardt, Natacha Rambova, Lillian Gish, and Eleonora Duse embraced Fortuny's free-flowing shapes and exotic patterns and colors. Sculptor Elena Sorolla García, Chinese American painter and writer Mai-mai

Sze, art collector Peggy Guggenheim, interior designer Elsie McNeill, and fashion designer Clarisse Coudert—who was married to Condé Nast, owner of *Vanity Fair* and *Vogue*—wore Fortuny. But even his most unconventional clients reserved the Delphos for at-home wear. The arc of fashion bends toward informality; the casual clothing of one generation becomes the formalwear of the next. Only years later did the Delphos become acceptable outside the house, as eveningwear.

Marcel Proust memorialized Fortuny in *A la recherche du temps perdu,* dressing Albertine Simonet and Madame de Guermantes in Fortuny gowns "swarmed with Arabic ornaments, like the Venetian palaces hidden like sultanas behind a screen of pierced stone." As Proust put it, the Spaniard's designs were "faithfully antique but markedly original." But neoclassicism and Orientalism (a term that, at the time, encompassed African, Middle Eastern, and Russian as well as Asian design influences) were not unique to Fortuny's work. They were also present in his contemporary Léon Bakst's costume designs for the Ballets Russes and in the clothing and textiles produced by the Wiener Werkstätte, whose cofounder, Josef Hoffmann, had visited Pompeii after winning the Prix de Rome in 1895.

Couturier Paul Poiret is remembered for his exuberant Orientalism, complete with jeweled turbans, minaret-shaped skirts, and billowing "harem" pantaloons. But his early gowns were high-waisted and uncorseted in the ancient Grecian mode. *Vogue* even hailed him as a "prophet of simplicity" in 1913. "I feel satisfied with my creations only if they give an impression of simple charm, of calm perfection comparable to that which is felt when standing before an antique statue," the designer claimed.[6] However, Poiret's vision of antiquity was filtered through the romanticized neoclassicism of the Directoire and Empire; he gave his vertically striped and pleated gowns names like "Joséphine" (after Joséphine Bonaparte) and "1811," and accessorized them with shawls, parasols, and bandeaus wrapped "à la Madame de Staël," named for Joséphine's contemporary, the writer Germaine de Staël (see Plate 2).

Along with his famous "1002nd Night" costume party of 1911, Poiret hosted a "Feasts of Bacchus" party in the summer of 1912. The three hundred guests wore fashionable Poiret gowns and tunics inspired by chitons, decorated with Greek key and Greek wave patterns, as well as more theatrical costumes, like the one worn by the bewigged designer himself. "I received them dressed as the Chryselephantine statue of Jove," Poiret recalled in his autobiography, "golden hair all curly, the golden beard, too, draped in ivory voile, and shod with buskins."

The Delphos was not just ahead of its time but timeless. Inspired by antiquity, it has never really gone out of style, a rare distinction in the fickle world of women's fashion. Those lucky enough to own them have kept and re-worn them for decades. In 1969, twenty years after the designer's death, socialite Gloria Vanderbilt posed for *Vogue* in her Fortunys, saying: "They are like one's skin. . . . They are so voluptuous, and sort of mold themselves to the body in a kind of marvelous way. Yet they are so very fragile, delicate . . . tender." *Dr. Zhivago* actress Geraldine Chaplin wore one of her mother's Delphos gowns and shawls in the 1979 movie *Mamá cumple 100 años*; she was filmed walking into the wind with her arms outstretched like the *Winged Victory of Samothrace* (see Plate 3). Actress Lauren Bacall wore a vintage red Delphos to the 1979 Oscars ceremony, and writer and philosopher Susan Sontag was buried in a copy of a

Fortuny dress in 2004. Instead of being hung on a hanger, Delphos gowns are stored twisted and coiled in their round boxes to preserve the pleats—"kept wrung like a skein of wool," as Lady Cooper said.[7] In closets and museums around the world, brilliantly colored Delphos gowns lie curled in the dark, like snakes waiting to strike.

At times of transition and uncertainty, women have returned again and again to the austere elegance of the ancient past, in search of archetypes of feminine power. Classical imagery was a feature of the suffrage pageants, processions, and pantomimes seen in both the United States and the United Kingdom as women organized to win the vote in the early twentieth century—elaborate theatrical spectacles that ensured these gatherings would be photographed and publicized. At the landmark 1913 Woman Suffrage Procession in Washington, D.C., the Ionic columns of the Treasury Department's south porch provided "an enchanting and appropriate setting for the Greek costumes of the allegorical characters" in a tableau representing Justice, Liberty, Hope, and other virtues, *The Birmingham News* reported. At a parade in Baltimore later the same year, women in Grecian gowns drove golden chariots representing states where women could vote. Many suffragists wore head-to-toe white, which represented purity and virtue in the movement's official iconography, as well as invoking classical statuary. It made an indelible visual impact and conveyed unity and respectability while being accessible to women of varying economic status. (Female politicians and members of Congress continue to wear white on important occasions today, in solidarity with the early suffragists.) Easily recognizable classical allusions lent the suffrage movement intellectual and moral authority; by dressing like goddesses and muses, the suffragists projected strength and heroism without appearing problematically masculine. (Joan of Arc was a popular suffragist symbol for the same reason.) Instead of engaging in angry protest, the suffragists aligned themselves with ancient symbols of grace, beauty, and intellect, suggesting that giving women the vote was not only virtuous and democratic but inevitable.

Classicism is an anti-fashion fashion statement, whether its simplicity is real—a tubular sheath—or a carefully constructed facsimile of haphazard drapery, buoyed by complex seaming and underpinnings that its designer took pains to hide or disguise. Its pared-down minimalism resets the clock and cleanses the palate, stripping fashion down to its essence—especially in response to periods of extreme sartorial excess, as happened in both the 1790s and the 1990s. The longevity of the Delphos proved to be self-perpetuating, as it inspired a host of imitations and homages from designers as diverse as Madeleine Vionnet, Halston, and Issey Miyake. While each of these reinterpretations approached antiquity from a unique viewpoint, they had several things in common, primarily draping, pleating, asymmetry, and the color white. Instead of zippers and buttons, they were fastened by brooches, ties, drawstrings, or perhaps a thin belt or cord. They were worn with appropriately ancient accessories—jewelry, headbands, sandals—and minimal undergarments.

The streamlined modernism of the early 1930s was rooted in neoclassicism; the somber, elegant architecture of the period mirrored columnar white evening gowns with severe but seductive lines in fluid matte fabrics that looked like cold marble rather than translucent linen. The style was especially attractive to women designers like Augusta Bernard, Madame

Grès, Maria Monaci Gallenga, and Vionnet, who used it to cel-
ebrate the natural contours of the female form. The escapist
and sometimes surreal fantasies that characterized 1930s fashion photography by Man Ray, Cecil Beaton, Horst P. Horst,
and their contemporaries turned models into mysterious and
otherworldly goddesses. Harry Yoxall, the longtime managing
director and chairman of Condé Nast, remembered how "our
Paris studios resounded with the noise of saws and hammers, as
joiners shaped and carpenters assembled details from the Par-
thenon or the Erechtheum, to set off the lovely fluted dresses"
in photo shoots. "The great couturiers are makers of colored
statues with living armatures, so to speak—the women who
wear their clothes. They are Pygmalions whose Galateas must
always come to life."[8] The interplay of fashion, ancient history,
and fine art gave these sensual designs a cerebral subtext.

No designer since Fortuny has been more attuned to the
classic aesthetic than Vionnet, who chose a woman standing
on an Ionic capital as her logo. "An artist in fabric," as fashion editor Carmel Snow called her, she pioneered the bias
cut—cutting across the grain of the material—which created
cling without the need for a patented pleating process. (She
commissioned unusually wide fabrics for this purpose and
kept distracting patterns and trimmings to a minimum.) She
never sketched, but draped and twisted her designs on a small
wooden mannequin set on a turntable; their minimal surface
decoration included embroidery motifs lifted from Greek vases.
Like a sculptor, she worked in three dimensions, paying as
much attention to the back of the gown as the front. Vionnet,
too, dressed Isadora Duncan, and her models went barefoot
like Duncan's dancers. She claimed that it was she, not Poiret,

who first banished the corset. Her gowns had no conspicuous undergarments or stiff linings. None were needed; Vionnet designed for tall, slender women and shooed anyone who
did not fit her physical ideal out of her grand salon—a fashion Pantheon decorated with friezes and doorways sculpted
by René Lalique and frescoes of women wearing Vionnet's
designs painted by Georges de Feure. In a famous 1931 series
of photographs for *Vogue*, George Hoyningen-Huene created
a bas-relief of model Sonia Colmer wearing Vionnet's flowing pyjamas; to achieve the flattened effect, Colmer posed on
a slanted board covered in black fabric, the folds in her gown
carefully pinned into place. In 1924, the *Gazette du bon ton* pronounced Vionnet's timeless clothes "above fashion."

The same could be said of the Grecian-style gowns designed by Vionnet's contemporary Madame Grès. "Probably
only Madame Grès herself can tell with certainty a magnifi-
cent long-sleeved pleated jersey dress from 1938, from one
made yesterday," fashion curator Madeleine Ginsburg noted in
1972.[9] Born Germaine Krebs, and also known professionally as
Madame Alix, Grès "wanted to be a sculptor" as a child. "For
me, working with fabric or stone is the same thing," she said.
"The procedure was quite different from anything I'd known,"
one of her models remembered, "for Grès folded, pinned, and
held the cloth against one, almost making the dress then and
there."[10] The designer created her "living sculptures" out of
double-width silk jersey, often in shades of white and gray, the
colors of marble and stone (see Plate 4).

In 1954, Willy Maywald photographed a Grès gown on a
model with one breast exposed; like the Venus de Milo, she
appeared as half woman, half skirt. Like Vionnet, Grès worked

in three dimensions, draping directly on the body. But she was always in control; her pleats were sewn into place, and her theatrical swags of fabric were anchored to invisible fitted understructures made by corsetière Alice Cadolle. Her gowns were as complex as Vionnet's, if less dependent on the bias cut; they were luxe rather than minimalist, with twists, ties, straps, peplums, and braided belts. Some were made of interwoven strips of fabric or cut away to allow glimpses of the torso; *Vogue* editor Bettina Ballard remembered one Grès evening ensemble with a bare midriff, "which was fashion at its most daring."[11] But for Grès, the ultimate goal was a seamless garment; at the 1939 World's Fair in New York, she presented a draped and cinched gown made of a single length of fabric.

In 1943, as the U.S. waged war on several fronts, ancient history offered both idealism and escapism. On Broadway, Mary Martin made her leading-lady debut playing a statue of the Roman goddess of love brought to life in modern-day New York in *One Touch of Venus*, a musical twist on the Pygmalion myth. The producer promised her that she would be "wearing the most beautiful clothes in the world." The Paris couturier Mainbocher—born Main Rousseau Bocher in Chicago—had returned to the U.S. when the war broke out, and he was recruited to design Martin's costumes, his first efforts for the stage. "Every time I walked onstage as Venus there was applause—for Main's clothes," the actress recalled in her autobiography. *Vogue* published a two-page spread featuring photos of Martin in all eight of her costumes, which included both "Grecian" gowns and contemporary clothes with antique touches like crisscrossing straps, cord belts, and "a huge jersey scarf which went on for about a block"; they also appeared in *Harper's Bazaar* and on the cover of *LIFE*. Statuesque in more ways than one, they gave the five-foot-three diva a suitably goddess-like stage presence; an upswept hairdo, plunging necklines, flesh-colored tights, and backless styles lengthened her silhouette. Instead of marble-like white, though, Martin wore graduated shades of pink; "Venus pink," inspired by the inside of the clamshell from which the mythical Venus emerged, enjoyed an unseasonal vogue that fall. Mainbocher, who continued to dress Martin on- and offstage, paid homage to the goddess by lining her costumes in pink silk.[12] In the 1948 film version of the musical, Ava Gardner would play the role of Venus, dressed by Orry-Kelly in a more traditional interpretation of Grecian costume: a toga-like white gown, wrapped and tied on one shoulder. "Ava Gardner had the most perfect figure I have ever dressed," the designer later told the *Detroit Free Press*. "She needed no underpinnings. . . . All I did . . . was to drape her form with white jersey."

In the aftermath of World War II, some couturiers turned to the classical look as a utopian antidote to the horrors of war. Molyneux and Lanvin were among those who attempted to revive the Empire waist, although their efforts were foiled by the success of Christian Dior's corseted and full-skirted New Look (see Chapter 6). Dior's pinched and padded silhouette was as far from Fortuny's clinging sheaths as possible, but he, too, produced evening gowns incorporating classical attributes and named after the Roman goddesses Venus and Juno. (The Venus gown was inspired by seashells, the Juno gown by peacock feathers.) Other designers gave an antiquated air to hourglass-shaped dresses with short jackets, shawls, or contrasting bodices suggesting a raised waistline.

If the simplicity of classical drapery did not translate easily to postwar haute couture, it was perfectly suited to Seventh Avenue's mass-produced ready-to-wear and sportswear, imparting a timeless quality to "The American Look." Women designers, especially, embraced the ease and egalitarianism of the classical idiom, rendered in inexpensive yet sturdy fabrics. While studying at Parsons Paris in the 1920s, Claire McCardell had snapped up Vionnet and Grès gowns at flea markets to disassemble and study. During and immediately after World War II, her cinched, corded, and wrapped dresses, skirts, and playsuits elevated humble materials like denim, mattress ticking, and nylon to Olympian heights of beauty and elegance; a cinched cotton sundress McCardell designed for Everfast in 1952 was printed with a Greek key pattern.[13] Like Fortuny and Vionnet, she was influenced by the uninhibited movement of modern dance, popularizing comfortable Capezio ballet shoes as fashionable flats. Another American disciple of Vionnet, Elizabeth Hawes, prioritized simplicity of line, freedom of movement, and quality of materials over embellishment, producing clothes that were both functional and comfortable. She gave her gowns cheekily classical names like "Pandora," "The Styx," and "Falernum," after a Roman wine. Her love of the antique grew out of her preference for clothes that were timeless, not trendy; she assured her clients that they could wear her dresses until they fell to pieces. Tina Leser, whose sportswear was inspired by her global travels, won a Coty Award for her "strapped-and-wrapped" silhouettes in 1945, including a draped white jersey dinner dress modeled on the Indian dhoti. In May 1945, *Vogue* described Leser's skirted swim dress of pleated and wrapped white Celanese rayon jersey as a "Greek goddess bathing suit, bare and flowing in marble folds—beautiful for all bodies this side celestial." The model wore metallic gold sandals and an upswept "Psyche-knot" coiffure.

First Lady Jacqueline Kennedy was known for wearing simple A-line and sheath dresses. But she had an unerring sense of history, and on one memorable occasion she went into full goddess mode, choosing a Grecian-inspired celadon silk jersey gown by Oleg Cassini for a 1962 White House dinner honoring forty-nine Nobel Prize winners as well as Pulitzer Prize winners, noted actors, and poet laureates. The Kennedy White House may have been nicknamed "Camelot," but on that night, it was a new Athens, bringing together the best minds in science, philosophy, art, and literature. "I think this is the most extraordinary collection of talent, of human knowledge, that has ever been gathered together at the White House, with the possible exception of when Thomas Jefferson dined alone," the president joked. The First Lady's dress completed the illusion of an evening at the Acropolis.

Most newspaper accounts of the event erroneously reported that the gown was made of chiffon—an understandable mistake given its lightness. The *Detroit Free Press* called it an "unusual draped gown of seafoam green." For her, it *was* an unusual choice; the asymmetrical neckline resembled a wrapped and tied garment, and the hue evoked the myth of Venus, rising from the sea on a scallop shell. Kennedy would repeat both the classical motif and the color in 1967, when she wore a flowing Valentino gown to a dinner at the Chamcar Mon Palace in Phnom Penh, Cambodia. Half toga, half sari, the gown also referenced the "sbai" or shoulder cloth of traditional Cambodian dress. This time, Kennedy bared one shoulder and arm (though it was clad in a long white glove). The ruffled edge of the seafoam-green satin gown was frosted with sparkling embroidery, like a breaking wave.

Kennedy's successor, Lady Bird Johnson, favored gowns by an actual Greek designer, George Stavropoulos, who had moved to New York in 1961 after marrying an American who worked for the U.S. Embassy in Athens. At a time when many American designers still looked to Paris for guidance, Stavropoulos was known for his diaphanous draped eveningwear evoking the classical statuary of his native land. His distinctive "goddess gowns" were modeled after togas, unbelted and unseamed, with layered panels of translucent chiffon, organza, and silk crêpe falling from one or both shoulders. Sensual but never scandalous, they were an elegant iteration of the caftans, dashikis, and other unstructured ethnic fashions popularized by the 1960s counterculture. Johnson notably chose two of his gowns for a visit to Bangkok, where they harmonized with the Thai court dress worn by her hostess, Queen Sirikit. Stavropoulos's loyal customers—who included Elizabeth Taylor and Maria Callas as well as Mrs. Johnson—defended his high prices by insisting that his clothes, inspired by antiquity, never went out of fashion.

James Galanos—born in Philadelphia to Greek immigrants—took a different approach to goddess dressing. His Spring 1970 collection featured bold, colorful prints of caryatids, Corinthian columns, centaurs, nymphs, satyrs, warriors, lions, and Greek letters by textile designer Tzaims Luksus. Instead of togas and chitons, he fashioned these sheer, fluid materials into flowing midi and maxi dresses designed to show off the oversized motifs; there wasn't a single short skirt in the collection. "If fashion looks all Greek to you at the moment, then you know a trend when you see one," *The Philadelphia Inquirer* quipped in its March 1970 review of the Galanos and Stavropoulos collections. "The ancient Greeks created an ideal of beauty and proportion that I don't think anyone has ever been able to improve upon, and I get a sense of that proportion and that kind of beauty frequently, particularly when he's draping a dress," Galanos model Natalie Tirrell explained. "There's almost an eternal feeling about it."[14]

It's no coincidence that vintage Fortuny gowns were particularly popular in the late 1960s and 1970s; they harmonized with the sleek, body-conscious minimalism of Halston, Calvin Klein, and Stephen Burrows. (A 1967 retrospective at the Los Angeles County Museum of Art undoubtedly fueled the Fortuny revival, as well.) Costume designer Irene Sharaff dressed Barbra Streisand in a vintage Fortuny Peplos in *Funny Girl* (1968), set just before World War I. "I thought the Fortuny dress was gorgeous," Streisand wrote in her 2010 book *My Passion for Design*. "Utterly simple—held together by a thin silk cord at the shoulders and very complex with that infinitesimal pleating. . . . No one has ever figured out how he did those tiny pleats. It's like Tiffany glass in a way. You can't quite duplicate it, although many people have tried." Indeed, Streisand persuaded Sharaff to make a duplicate of the dress in pink for her to wear in her "A Happening in Central Park" concert, which took place during *Funny Girl*'s filming.

Halston sexed up classicism with bare shoulders, plunging necklines, and high slits to reveal the legs. He worked in clinging cashmere knits and silk jerseys as well as transparent silk chiffons. Model Lauren Hutton wore his gown to the

1975 Academy Awards ceremony, accessorized by a simple gold belt and a conspicuous lack of jewelry or undergarments. Composed of a pastel rainbow of rectangular chiffon panels, it looked as though it might have been draped and belted in place rather than sewn. Just as the Delphos was accented by cords and beads handmade by Fortuny's artisans, Halston's deceptively simple gowns were meant to be set off by Elsa Peretti's sculptural metal belts and jewelry.

In the 1980s, Mary McFadden and Roberto Capucci both experimented with Fortuny-style pleats, but while Capucci's architectural clothes distorted the body rather than freeing it, McFadden embraced the classical aesthetic. The former fashion editor and publicist launched her eponymous label in 1975. With Fortuny's inventiveness, she created her own synthetic fabric, dubbed "marii," which was manufactured in Australia, then hand-dyed in Japan and machine-pleated in the U.S.—all so it would fall "like liquid gold on the body, as if it were Chinese silk," McFadden wrote in her 2012 memoir. The designer indulged in self-consciously "antique" details like laurel leaves, floral wreaths, macramé cords, turbans, shawls, and woven belts. She had her models photographed under the pediment of the New York Public Library, like Greek caryatids. A 1983 *Vogue* layout featured model Iman wearing McFadden's designs next to a marble bust perched on a fluted white column and an enormous white plaster amphora, a two-handled jar. But McFadden's characteristic pleats appeared more crinkled, stiff, and shiny than Fortuny's, like crêpe paper, and her gowns often had modern touches like puffed sleeves, natural waistlines, and cabbage-like ruffles and rosettes; bands of densely beaded and sequined embroidery; and other decorative flourishes. As a result, they are instantly recognizable as being from the 1980s rather than Fortuny's era, much less classical antiquity.

Issey Miyake, the experimental designer who first showed finely pleated garments in his Spring/Summer 1989 collection, is often compared to Fortuny. But while Fortuny used Japanese silk treated and pleated with a patented process, Miyake works in polyester, whose thermoplastic properties allow it to hold its pleats even with washing. And, unlike Fortuny, Miyake makes oversized garments and then pleats them, rather than working with pre-pleated fabric, a process he calls "garment pleating." This is not just a technical choice but a philosophical one; for Miyake, the pleats give identical, mass-produced clothing individuality, enabling them to mold themselves to the wearer's body. In 1993, he introduced his "Pleats Please" line to explore the possibilities of pleated garments, often using the pleats to create volume rather than reduce it. "Western clothes are cut and shaped with the body as the starting point," the designer has said. "Japanese clothes start with the fabric." Miyake is interested in the intersection of the two; this cross-cultural perspective is, perhaps, the most Fortuny-like aspect of his work, along with an interest in producing versatile, comfortable, easy-to-store clothes for modern living.

In 1996, Miyake launched the Pleats Please Guest Artist series and invited contemporary artists to produce limited-edition collections. Japanese multimedia artist Yasumasa Morimura created a series of three dresses incorporating Jean-Auguste-Dominique Ingres's neoclassical painting *La Source* of 1856, depicting a nude woman pouring water out of a clay amphora, superimposed with an inverted half-length photo of the artist on the bottom half, his head and torso draped in red netting (see Plate 5). The digital collage was then manipulated to correct for the distortion imposed by the pleating process. The dresses are visually bisected, so it appears that both the wearer and the nude figure are wearing red skirts; the anatomy of the Ingres figure is only slightly misaligned with the wearer's anatomy: breasts, abdomen, feet. The juxtaposition destabilizes traditional binaries—male and female, East and West, naked and clothed—and blurs the boundaries between art, artist, and audience. This visual and metaphorical layering of ancient inspiration and modern technology questions the very nature of the dress itself.

A century or so after Fortuny fashioned his first Delphos, the classical look was back in the spotlight for another notable beginning: the inauguration of America's first Black president, Barack Obama. For the 2009 inaugural balls, First Lady Michelle Obama chose a white gown of diaphanous silk chiffon embellished with three-dimensional, crystal-studded flowers, custom-made for her by Jason Wu, a then-unknown twenty-six-year-old designer (see Plate 6). Just as the suffrage movement had harnessed the symbolism of white, Wu intended the color to represent hope; Obama had run on a platform of "hope and change." But it also evoked the marble statuary (and, by extension, the democratic principles) of ancient Greece and Rome, as did the gown's unusual construction. Though most journalists described it as "one-shouldered," its neckline was more complicated than that. A band of fabric circled the bodice; it was ruched and twisted, Vionnet-style, at the center, then angled over one shoulder with toga-like asymmetry. (At a time when sleeveless dresses were still banned in the House of Representatives, Obama frequently bared her famously toned arms.)

Similar variations on this tied-and-twisted theme appeared in Wu's Fall 2009 collection, presented at New York Fashion Week just a month after the inauguration. Wu said the collection was inspired by a book of fairy tales illustrated by Arthur Rackham. One of the leading British illustrators of the early twentieth century, Rackham was strongly influenced by the Pre-Raphaelites and the English Arts and Crafts Movement— the same art movements that had revived neoclassical styles in the late 1800s, seduced by their beauty, simplicity, and ease of movement. The Delphos charioteer had come full circle.

2

THE TENNIS SKIRT
Changing the Game

In 1919, twenty-year-old Frenchwoman Suzanne Lenglen made her Wimbledon debut in a shockingly skimpy ensemble: a V-neck dress with short sleeves and a calf-length pleated skirt. A floppy hat covered her cropped hair. She rolled her white silk stockings above her knees because garters would have constrained her legs. She didn't wear a corset. She didn't even wear a petticoat. Though the press called her outfit "indecent," Lenglen went on to win the tournament, becoming the first non–English speaker to do so. It marked the beginning of a bracing new era for Wimbledon, which had been on a four-year hiatus during World War I, and for women's tennis in general. Lenglen would dominate the international tennis scene until her withdrawal from amateur tennis in 1926, winning five Wimbledon championships as well as two French titles and three Olympic medals. Her winning streak made tennis history, while also altering the course of fashion history.

At a time when female players typically wore the same ankle-length skirts and high-necked, long-sleeved blouses on and off the court, Lenglen's attire was as revolutionary as her overhand serve and penchant for chugging cognac between sets; never before in Western history had women's legs been on display. As the teens turned into the twenties, her short-sleeved dress gave way to sleeveless dresses, and her linen hat to a much-copied headband, dubbed "the Lenglen bandeau." Instead of lace-up boots with shapely heels, she wore flat, rubber-soled "Lenglen shoes" of white doeskin. Originally chosen for comfort on the tennis court, these chic, practical styles soon spilled over into women's everyday wardrobes. At the height of her career, Lenglen was the most famous female athlete in the world, a mainstay of the sports pages, the gossip columns, and the fashion magazines alike. By 1926, when Queen Mary presented her with a medal to mark the fiftieth anniversary of the Wimbledon Championships, it was the young athlete—dressed in a sleeveless white dress with a short pleated skirt, a green sweater-vest, "Lenglen shoes," and cropped hair anchored by her trademark bandeau—and not the venerable lilac-clad queen who was the global fashion influencer.

Perhaps more than any other sport, women's tennis seems to attract (and provoke) fashion drama. That's partly because it has such a long history; the All England Lawn Tennis and Croquet Club, which hosts the Wimbledon Championships, was founded in 1868. The sport clings to its time-honored traditions, and nowhere more so than at Wimbledon, where you can always count on finding strawberries and cream, ad-free courts, royal spectators, and a game-free Middle Sunday. The

FIGURE 5. Suzanne Lenglen, dressed in her trademark bandeau and short skirt, curtsies to Queen Mary at Wimbledon in 1926. (*Bibliothèque nationale de France*)

"gentlemen" and "ladies" still play on grass, as they have since the birth of the modern game in 1873.

This reverence for heritage also applies to dress. The concept of "tennis whites" dates back to the game's Victorian origins. White was thought to keep players cool and hide unsightly sweat stains; if it presented laundering challenges, they were of little concern to the leisured elites who played the game. When the All England Club first opened, women were not allowed to play there, and the only sartorial guidance was: "Gentlemen are requested not to play in their shirtsleeves when ladies are present." But when women began to compete in the Wimbledon Championships in 1884, the question of what to wear took on fresh urgency. To this day, Wimbledon has the most stringent dress code on the pro tour; even some spectators are subject to outfit guidelines. In 1963, as traditions of all kinds showed signs of crumbling, Wimbledon instituted a "predominantly white" dress code, revising it to "almost entirely white" in 1995. It also stipulated that players should wear "suitable tennis attire"—a much more subjective and slippery rubric.

In a sport long associated with country houses and country clubs, the very notion of "suitability" was bound up with social class and race as well as gender. (Many of those clubs banned Black and Jewish members; not only the clothes were white.) Tennis wasn't a man's game that adapted to admit women; from the beginning, "it was revolutionary in having women and men participate together, actually playing on the same arena and hitting the ball at one another."[1] Since the days when "suitable tennis attire" for women consisted of bustles, corsets, gloves, and sun hats, female players have struggled to strike a balance between performance and propriety. A tennis manual of 1903, *Lawn Tennis at Home and Abroad,* advised female players to look their best, "for all eyes are on them. Many an onlooker understands nothing about the game, and the next thing generally is to criticise the player and her looks." The tennis court was also one of the few places where single men and women could socialize unchaperoned; Major Walter Clopton Wingfield, who patented the modern rules of lawn tennis, promoted the game as a venue for courtship of the romantic variety. Looking good was essential to making a love match.

But even as women's tennis clothes diverged from their everyday dress, female players came under increased scrutiny. Maud Watson, who won the first ladies' championship in 1884, raised eyebrows with her ankle-length skirt. The 1887 champion, Lottie Dod, got away with a calf-length skirt because she was just fifteen years old, but she was expected to wear her skirts longer as she grew up. "I don't think that our old-fashioned dresses were as much of a handicap as people now suppose," she remembered in her seventies. "But it was difficult to run backward to volley a high ball as one feared treading on one's skirt."[2] When American player May Sutton bared even more leg in 1905, she was forced to lower her hemline before being allowed to play; her short-sleeved blouse also caused comment. Her sister and fellow competitor Violet Sutton complained: "It's a wonder we could move at all. Do you want to know what we wore? A long undershirt, pair of drawers, two petticoats, white linen corset cover, duck shirt, shirtwaist, long white silk stockings, and a floppy hat. We were soaking wet when we finished a match."[3]

As the genteel "pat-ball" of the Victorian Era was replaced

by a more athletic, energetic game, tennis dress was slow to adapt; competitive female players continued to wear corsets and confining skirts well into the 1920s. "When one recalls the tennis dress of a few years ago, with long skirts and long sleeves, one wonders how women ever managed to play at all," wrote reigning world champion Helen Wills in her 1928 book *Tennis.* "How could any one run with skirts down to her ankles and her waist tightly confined in corsets?" She added: "The ideal length is at the centre of the knee-cap. . . . Skirts shorter than this . . . give no greater freedom, and are usually unattractive-looking." In September 1934, *Vogue* conceded: "It is all very well to have a fourteen-inch waist if you are going to drive sedately in a smart Victoria, but the case is greatly altered if you are bent on beating your record at golf or taking a forty-mile ride on a bike."

Lenglen's unfettered waist and short(ish) skirts marked the beginning of the end of restrictive clothing for sportswomen. The American player Bill Tilden derided Lenglen's signature style as "a cross between a prima donna and a streetwalker." But *Vogue* praised it as "extraordinarily chic in the freedom, the suitability, and the excellence of its simple lines." And Lenglen's contemporary, American champion Elizabeth Ryan, said that "all women players should go on their knees in thankfulness to Suzanne for delivering them from the tyranny of corsets." Lenglen became a style icon off the court as well, making sportif clothes a chic choice for streetwear. Tennis clothes began to appear in fashion magazines like *Vogue* and the *Journal des dames et des modes,* with familiar designer labels. When Lenglen visited America in August 1921, *The Boston Globe* devoted as many column inches to her wardrobe as to her game: "Dressed in a simple one-piece linen dress that reaches only to her knees and is cut off short above the elbow, with her hair tied up in a wide sash of red or orange silk, with the lightest of cloth sandals on her feet, she is indeed a picturesque figure, even before she makes a shot." Lenglen's fashion influence was especially potent in America. Her short, sleeveless, body-skimming dresses and separates showed off what was widely considered to be the American woman's greatest asset: her long-limbed, athletic figure. "Surely the American woman has never known such amazing activity as in this first quarter of the twentieth century," *Vogue* observed in May 1923, "and never—not even in the perilous bicycle era—has she dressed so carefully as now for the activities of her preference."

Lenglen's tennis clothes were made by Jean Patou, who had opened his Paris couture house in 1919, after serving in World War I. In 1920, Patou's sister and muse, Madeleine, married Raymond Barbas, a member of the French national tennis team. Barbas introduced the fledgling couturier to Lenglen, then fresh from her Wimbledon debut. Although Lenglen, with her bad teeth and beaky nose, was no beauty, she had innate style and confidence. She would become Patou's best model and advertisement, on and off the court, and inspired a generation of Frenchwomen to take up tennis, or at least dress as if they had. Both Patou and Lenglen were decades ahead of their time in recognizing the symbiotic relationship between fashion and sport, and both had a genius for manipulating the media. In November 1924, Patou created a stir on both sides of the Atlantic by advertising for American fashion models to come to work for him in Paris, because his American clients wanted to see his clothes on leggy American figures. He milked the *American Idol*–style selection process for months' worth of free publicity.

Previously, sportswear had been considered an English specialty. The outdoorsy English country lifestyle revolved around riding and shooting in tailored tweeds. But World War I forced many Frenchwomen into more active lives; they began driving cars, and they demanded mobility in their wardrobes, as well. But these clothes had to be in step with fashion; mannish tweeds need not apply. In the 1920s, as more women (and men) took up leisure activities like golf and tennis, skiing and skating, the line between clothing designed for sport and "sportswear"—a term coined in the late nineteenth century but increasingly applied to soft, casual clothing rather than athletic gear—began to blur. A fit physique and a suntan—once the marks of a rural laborer—now signified someone with the time and money for trips to the Riviera and Alpine ski resorts. (*Vogue* noted a trend for "sunburn color" stockings in May 1926.) As professional French athletes like Lenglen found success on the world stage, the market for sportswear expanded to include these well-heeled amateurs.

Patou—who also dressed Lenglen's American rival Helen Wills—was not the only Paris couturier to target this lucrative new audience. Both Coco Chanel and Madeleine Vionnet opened special departments dedicated to sportswear, and even more staid houses like Lanvin and Paquin began including a handful of sportswear "models" in each collection. "A few years ago the sports costume was ignored by the French couturier," *Vogue* noted in 1922. "Now it appears in the collection of almost every house." Chanel designed the costumes for Serge Diaghilev's 1924 sport-themed ballet, *Le Train Bleu,* set on the French

Riviera and featuring the kind of swimming, golf, and tennis ensembles sold in her boutiques. In 1927, Hermès created a tennis tunic embroidered with racquets. Lenglen became "sports directress" of the Yvonne May fashion house in 1930, after her retirement; in 1933, French men's champion René "Le Croc" Lacoste parlayed his success on the court into a fashion business that is still going strong today. Fred Perry, Ted Tinling, and Alice Marble followed suit, launching their own fashion lines. Meanwhile, leaders of couture's old guard like Doucet, Chéruit, and Poiret saw their business plummet as their opulent, heavily embellished gowns fell out of style, along with their longstanding customer base of pampered courtesans. As couturière Louise Boulanger complained to fashion editor Carmel Snow, "The day tennis came in, the demimondaine went out, and fashion with her."

Patou made all kinds of gowns, but he was best known for his sportswear: simple silhouettes in utilitarian fabrics with menswear details, like Chanel's, but designed for movement. (Had he not died prematurely in 1936, his name might be as familiar as Chanel's today; in Anita Loos's damning opinion, "Patou made Chanel look like a milliner.") Like Fortuny, Patou used pleats along with supple, stretchy fabrics like silk and wool jersey and tricot to facilitate movement while maintaining a slim, clean line. His clothes were radical in their simplicity, enlivened only by geometric patterns and embroideries inspired by Cubism, Art Deco, and folk costumes. (His eveningwear was just as streamlined, but with richer fabrics and embellishments.) His menswear-inspired knitted cardigans— long-sleeved, short-sleeved, or sleeveless—were worn by spectators and sportswomen alike. Patou's characteristic modernity extended from his clothes to his atelier, equipped with an elevator and a lighted stage for photography.

Though white was still the standard in competitions, Lenglen popularized rose and green Patou dresses accessorized with jackets, sweaters, cloche hats, and headbands. These sporting ensembles were "miracles of chic and convenience," *Vogue* declared in May 1923. "She may, if she likes, wear them all day long, progressing from breakfast to golf, golf to lunch, lunch to tennis, tennis to tea, without the necessity of changing anything but her shoes."

In 1924, Patou opened a shop dedicated to bathing costumes and sportswear in the seaside resort town of Deauville. A few months later, he opened a second one on the French Riviera. (He launched the first suntan oil, Huile de Chaldée, in 1927.) And, in 1925, on his brother-in-law's advice, he opened Le Coin des Sports, a boutique adjacent to his Paris premises specializing in clothing and equipment for tennis, golf, riding, fishing, and swimming, displayed in appropriately decorated rooms. Lenglen became what's now known as a brand ambassador; she may have been the first athlete to align herself with a fashion designer, though she was hardly the last. The Monte Carlo correspondent for the Universal Service called her an "outside mannequin," explaining: "Sport clothes . . . have become as elaborate as afternoon and evening gowns, obliging sport devotees to invest considerable amounts . . . to rig themselves out for tennis. A different sweater and scarf are generally donned for each game, pale green and beige being the predominant colors because they are favored by Mlle. Lenglen."

Sportswriters devoted column inches to the "Tennis Tigress of France" and her wardrobe. "Mlle. Lenglen wore a bright orange bandeau, with a silken sweater of lighter orange shade, which she never removed during the match," the European edition of *The Chicago Tribune and the Daily News* reported in June 1926, when Lenglen faced Californian Mary Browne on the clay courts of the Racing Club in the Bois de Boulogne. "The French net empress had the latest Parisienne makeup, with crimsoned lips, mascara on her eyes giving her a vivid contrast with pale Mary Browne, who played in the simplest white costume, arms bare to the shoulders, and without the slightest touch of cosmetics." Lenglen won the match, "with silken skirts flying."

The fashion press covered Lenglen with equal enthusiasm. A May 1926 *Vogue* "Guide to Chic for Tennis" noted that Lenglen preferred to play in "a white crêpe de chine sleeveless dress designed by Jean Patou. Over it, when the game is finished, she wears a green cardigan sweater." In August 1926, Lenglen wore Patou's pleated white silk tennis dress (paired with two layered cardigans and her trademark bandeau) in a French *Vogue* spread. The next page featured evening gowns made with similar knife pleats. Lenglen was back in American *Vogue* a few months later, under the headline "Suzanne Lenglen Shows How to Dress for Tennis." The article noted approvingly: "Her Jean Patou sports costumes are correct and chic on the court and after the game." Indeed, all the clothes featured were by Patou, "whose sports clothes have an outstanding chic and are in great demand among smart women." A few months after that, Lenglen modeled Patou's navy velvet coat trimmed with blue fox fur in *Les modes*; the only thing it had in common with tennis clothes was its abbreviated length, displaying Lenglen's now-famous legs.

Lenglen and her slim-hipped, short-skirted Patou clothes helped to make the androgynous, athletic "garçonne"—the French equivalent of the flapper—the fashionable ideal. Simply constructed of tubes and cubes, they were easy for home dress-makers to reproduce, making the sportif look accessible to a much wider market beyond couture buyers. (Indeed, one perennial criticism of flapper fashions was that they blurred the difference between the rich and the poor.) Lenglen's abbreviated hemlines and flat-soled shoes made ankles the new erogenous zone; ads for shoes designed to "slenderize" stout ankles began to appear in fashion magazines. In 1917, *Vogue* predicted that a new French fashion for diamond anklets "will now be the aspiration of all fortunate possessors of pretty slender ankles." A few years later, the magazine lamented that black stockings were no longer fashionable, since, paired with black shoes, they could "mitigate the impression" of thick ankles. Yet others blamed Lenglen for encouraging women to ruin their figures with exercise. In 1925, an annual "dainty ankle" competition in London was canceled because "tennis playing and other sports . . . had killed the shapely ankle, which had not yet shown any tendency of coming back," the Associated Press reported in a widely circulated story.

After Lenglen retired, tennis clothes began to diverge from street clothes once again. Fashionable hemlines dropped to mid-calf, while tennis skirts grew shorter and shorter. Bias-cut gowns, puffed sleeves, and floral prints had no place on the court, yet female athletes continued to set trends that had far-reaching effects for everyday dress. On June 23, 1931, Joan Lycett played at Wimbledon with bare legs, rather than white or nude stockings. But this transgression was nothing compared to that of her opponent. Spanish player Lilí Álvarez—"well known, not only for her tennis but also for her extremely chic appearance on the courts," per *Vogue*—wore Elsa Schiaparelli's "divided skirt," a garment she had already road-tested at the French Open. Though her knees were covered and her calves were sheathed in stockings, Álvarez was, technically, the first woman to play the tournament in shorts. "Old ladies gasped and old gentlemen gurgled as the comely Spanish player pranced about," *The New York Times* tutted. While they failed to catch on in the tennis world, similar culottes soon became a staple of 1930s fashion.

It wasn't long before actual shorts appeared on the court. A March 1926 article on tennis fashion in *The Paris Times* included a photo of "what are called 'shorts,' worn with a small skirt as a covering." (Both the "shorts" and the wrap-style skirt were knee-length.) But it would be several years before professional players adopted them, sans skirts. British player Henry "Bunny" Austin was the first man to wear shorts on the court, at the U.S. National Championship in 1932, and at Wimbledon the following year. "I expected a fuss there, but there was none," Austin told the *Boston Globe* years later, in 1997. "I don't know why we put up with long flannel trousers for so long." Naturally, there was more of a fuss when female players began wearing them soon thereafter. In 1938, Father Clement Parsons, the parish priest of St. Albans, complained to the *Daily Mirror* that the shorts worn by female players at Wimbledon were "offensive to the ordinary standards of Christian morality" and encouraged "sensuality among young men." California-born competitor Alice Marble, who was known for her especially short "American-style" shorts, found his objections "most amusing. . . . I used to wear skirts, but what happens when the wind blows?" Another American convert to shorts, Helen Hull Jacobs, told *The New York Times* in 1936 that they "improve my game and all the girls say the same. I have lost many points through my racquet catching in my skirt." In July 1948, *Holiday Magazine* declared that "the only controversy is that of shorts versus tennis dress"—a debate that raged at country clubs and public courts as well as on the pro tour.

Yet shorts proved to be a passing fad in women's tennis; presumably, they weren't comfortable enough to justify the controversy they generated. The 1930s, 1940s, and 1950s were the era of the "Glamour Girls of Tennis," as the *Mirror* dubbed them: tall, leggy players with movie-star good looks and wardrobes to match. Both Marble and Jacobs set trends in hats and evening gowns as well as sportswear. American Gertrude "Gorgeous Gussie" Moran wrote a fashion column, "Togs & Tennis," for *American Lawn Tennis* magazine. In 1936, British player Kay Stammers—who had reportedly turned down a contract offered by a Hollywood studio—wore a leopard-skin coat onto the court at the Surrey Hard Court Championships. Not to be outdone, Moran began to sport leopard-print and ruffled underpants under short white dresses, rendering them even more scandalous than shorts.

"No one ever knew what they wore underneath in those days," tennis player turned tennis fashion designer Ted Tinling, who made Moran's outfits, told the *Orlando Sentinel* in 1988. "No one would ever ask." Thanks to Moran's abbreviated hemline, they didn't have to. When Moran flashed lace-trimmed white panties at Wimbledon in 1949, the tournament organizers accused her of "bringing vulgarity and sin into tennis."

FIGURE 6. Gertrude "Gorgeous Gussie" Moran's tennis skirts were short enough to reveal lace-trimmed or leopard-print panties. (*Herald Examiner Collection / Los Angeles Public Library*)

(Others were more forgiving: a racehorse, an aircraft, and a restaurant's special sauce were named after her.) Tinling, who had acted as an official Wimbledon host for twenty-three years, was banned from the event for decades. Though skirts only got shorter, underpants remained controversial. Wimbledon expanded its all-white dress code to include accessories in

2014, after Tatiana Golovin and Serena Williams wore colorful knickers under their white dresses.

Paris couturiers began paying attention to tennis again when France's Françoise Dürr started racking up Grand Slams in the late 1960s. Pierre Cardin, Pierre Balmain, and André Courrèges (an avid player of pelota, a Basque game similar to tennis) produced tennis clothes for men and women alike. The dawn of the Open Era in 1968 saw prize purses swell and tennis explode as a popular pastime. In May 1971, *Vogue* declared tennis "the smash sport of the seventies," noting that 4,500 new courts were being built in the U.S. each year. Many of these were indoor courts, turning the quintessential summer pastime into a year-round activity.

Tinling had continued to transform the staid world of tennis clothes by introducing color, unusual materials, flashy trimmings, and flattering silhouettes; he designed an ostrich-feather miniskirt for Lea Pericoli in 1964 and put Dürr in Wimbledon's first halter dress in 1973. "I could see the unbelieving eyes and the nudging that went on in the committee box the day she wore the dress," he wrote in *The New York Times* in 1977. "I could imagine they felt this was a forerunner to the topless dress, and a whole specter of topless dresses must have come up in their minds when they realized they had no rules at that time against the dress."

When Bobby Riggs challenged Billie Jean King to a televised "Battle of the Sexes," she turned to Tinling for a dress. After King declared his original design to be too scratchy, Tinling substituted a backup dress of blue and menthol green—in homage to Virginia Slims, the sponsor of the women's tour, and King's signature blue suede Adidas tennis shoes. On the morning of the match, he frantically sewed rhinestones around the neckline, worried that the harsh lights of the Houston Astrodome would wash King out on camera. He wanted the 30,000 spectators and television audience of 50 million to pay attention to the history-making match. King won easily in straight sets, proving not just that a woman could beat a man but that she could do it in a dress. At the age of eleven, King had been left out of a group photo at a junior tournament because she was wearing home-sewn shorts instead of a skirt—an indignity she never forgot.

Tinling confessed: "I don't know why tennis clothes have the capacity to cause such tremendous emotions among men."[4] But cultural debates over women's fashion and bodies had always played out on the tennis court; in the era of women's lib and unisex dressing, the stakes were perilously high. When American player Anne White asked her sponsor, Pony, to design a white spandex bodysuit to keep her legs warm in the chilly English weather at Wimbledon in 1985, her unconventional attire drew jeers and whistles from the crowd. White's opponent, Pam Shriver, complained to officials after the match was suspended due to darkness; it was "the most bizarre, stupid-looking thing I've ever seen on a tennis court," she told a UPI reporter. Although the formfitting garment conformed to the "predominantly white" rule, the tournament referee agreed that it stretched the definition of "suitable tennis attire." When play resumed the next day, White's bodysuit was on the cover of every newspaper, but she wore a traditional tennis skirt.

Tinling declared White's bodysuit "the next logical step" in women's tennis attire, yet, once again, pants and shorts failed to displace the traditional tennis skirt. When Serena Williams wore a *Black Panther*–inspired Nike catsuit at the 2018 French Open, a similar controversy erupted. The outfit prompted a swift rule change to ban bodysuits at the Grand Slam, followed by a public outcry. "One must respect the game and the place," French Tennis Federation president Bernard Giudicelli told *Tennis* magazine—a statement that many interpreted as both racist and sexist. Williams had recently given birth to her daughter, Alexis, and the sleek compression suit was designed to prevent post-pregnancy blood clots; Williams said it made her feel like a superhero. King herself weighed in, tweeting: "The policing of women's bodies must end." As King astutely perceived, the ban was as much about the sexualization of Williams's body—revealed by the skintight suit—as about her dress. In response, the Women's Tennis Association altered its dress code to explicitly allow leggings and compression shorts without a skirt for its 2019 season; however, the WTA doesn't govern the Grand Slam.

A few months later, at the U.S. Open, Williams—who, with her sister Venus, had a long history of wearing boundary-pushing, trendsetting tennis clothes—made it clear that she would not let tournament organizers dictate what she wears on the court. Instead of pants, she chose lavender and black tutu dresses custom-made by Off-White founder, the late Virgil Abloh, in collaboration with Nike (see Plate 7). The dresses appeared to bare one shoulder, though the shoulder was actually covered with nude fabric, to prevent the dress from falling down during play. Williams completed the outfits with compression fishnet tights and sparkly silver NikeCourt Flare sneakers. Her choice of Abloh, a Black designer, was surely deliberate. When she returned to the French Open the following year, she wore another Abloh-designed crop top and skirt emblazoned with the words MOTHER, GODDESS, QUEEN, CHAMPION, in both French and English, proving that she didn't have to wear pants to make a statement.

Debates over women's tennis clothes matter partly because they are a reliable indicator of wider, off-court trends, in values as well as in dress. Athletic wear tends to forecast fashion, introducing high-tech materials and aerodynamic silhouettes that later migrate to everyday dress. Tennis clothing, which is unique to individual players and changes from match to match, has much greater potential to launch trends than, say, baseball or soccer team uniforms. One hundred years ago, tennis brought us shorter skirts, heels, and hairstyles, and less restrictive undergarments. Today it launches trends such as catsuits, unicorn hair, and athletic clothes made from recycled ocean plastic, like those Stella McCartney designed for Wimbledon in 2019.

Perhaps the question, then, is not why tennis players still wear skirts but why other elite women athletes don't. "They allow for so much movement," Venus Williams told *The Wall Street Journal* in 2021. "When you're lunging to return a shot or sprinting up to the net, it's critical that your outfit moves with you and lets you pivot, leap, or reach." Once, skirts were the norm for all kinds of physical exertion, from genteel pastimes like croquet and golf to the more energetic pursuits of baseball, basketball, and boxing. Today, only tennis players, figure skaters, and field hockey players regularly wear skirts in competition. Indeed, Puma was widely ridiculed in 2009 when it included wraparound skorts in a fashion show of its uniforms for the short-lived Women's Professional Soccer league. Though not intended to be worn on the field, the skorts were derided as a misguided attempt to feminize the sport and its players, reminiscent of the pastel dresses designed for the World War II–era All-American Girls Professional Baseball League. They were never seen again.

More than skirts, however, women's tennis, skating, and field hockey share long histories. International figure skating competitions, like tennis tournaments, began in the late nineteenth century, and they were often coed; women competed alongside men at the Olympics in 1908, when figure skating made its first appearance. Field hockey has even more ancient roots; the modern rules were codified in the 1880s, and the first women's clubs were founded around the same time. Significantly, all three sports were played outdoors, so wearing bloomers or a gym suit was not an option, as it was for sports women played in gymnasiums at the time. Their dress-centered dress codes are reminders of a time when women didn't just play with the boys but changed the game.

3

THE LITTLE
BLACK DRESS

Women in Uniform

*V*ogue called it a "Ford among dresses." Like the Model T, Coco Chanel's little black dress—which the magazine featured in its October 1, 1926, issue—was reliable, (relatively) affordable, and ubiquitous.

Above all, however, the comparison evoked its color. In his 1922 autobiography, Henry Ford recalled telling his management team that "any customer can have a car painted any color that he wants so long as it is black." Though the first Model Ts came in a handful of colors, from 1914 to 1925 they were only produced in black—which Ford preferred due to black paint's low cost, durability, and faster drying time. The LBD and the Model T were both icons of modernity, ushering in a new way of life that was both stripped down and sped up.

Chanel's version was called the Model 817. It was made of solid black crêpe de chine except for a discreet white zigzag at the cuff; an *X* formed of tiny pin tucks enlivened the stark

FIGURE 7. Chanel's "Ford"—as illustrated in *Vogue* in October 1926—was black but hardly basic, with subtly flattering pin tucks and white zigzag details at the cuff. (*Bocher / Condé Nast / Shutterstock.com*)

palette and imposed an hourglass silhouette on the boxy garment. With its low waist and short (meaning knee-length) skirt, it skimmed the body rather than shaping it, highlighting the slim, androgynous figure that was the fashionable ideal of the Roaring Twenties. But even as Chanel bared the legs, she compensated by hiding the arms in long, narrow sleeves, and thus "controverted the trend of two centuries."[1] Its only ornament, a string of pearls, stood out in sharp relief against the black fabric. A similar black crepella model appeared in *Vogue*'s next issue. "Few frocks achieve such sudden and great popularity as this one," the magazine noted.

Vogue predicted—correctly—that the little black dress would become a uniform: "the frock that all the world will wear." At a time when most men—from bankers to baseball umpires—still wore three-piece suits every day, the LBD offered a female equivalent: simple, practical, versatile, consistent. It was both serious and sporty, appropriate for women's increasingly active and public lifestyles. It had all the ease and modernity of Chanel's tennis clothes (see Chapter 2), but no one could mistake it for sportswear; the color announced that it meant business. For eveningwear, there were sleeveless versions in chiffon, lace, or sequins; Chanel was "famed for her black chiffons," *Vogue* noted, "a little bit of nothing, yet a masterpiece."[2]

Chanel was not the first designer to think of making little black dresses; Madeleine Vionnet and Maison Premet had produced similar styles in the early 1920s. But they were still noteworthy novelties in 1926. Today, black is associated with all things cool and chic. "Black is the most slimming of all colors," Christian Dior declared in his *Little Dictionary of Fashion* (1954). "It is the most flattering. You can wear black at any time. You can wear it at any age. You can wear it for almost any occasion. I could write a book about black." It's such a beloved fashion staple that major trends are jokingly described as "the new black." It's an emblem of both culture and counterculture: artists, beatniks, punks, Goths, hipsters, and Hells Angels. It's respectable or rebellious, depending on the context; it can go from a funeral to a cocktail party. A black dress on a debutante, or a bride, or a child still carries some shock value. In 1926, the little black dress had the same effect.

It may be hard to believe that black has not always been in style, but you'd have to look back several centuries to find a fashion moment comparable to the one Chanel sparked. Black took hold as a fashion color in the mid-sixteenth century. During the Renaissance, black was the height of elegance and luxury. High-quality, colorfast black dye was expensive; Spanish and Dutch princes (and merchant princes) and their wives wore black to show off their wealth. But as those empires fell and France (with its brilliant flowered silks) and England (with its richly saturated dyed wools) grew in political, military, and dynastic power, black faded from fashion. It was increasingly reserved for mourning—a lucrative branch of the fashion industry in its own right. Mourning was a matter of etiquette as much as dress; there were specified forms and intervals of mourning for different family members, and entire nations mourned members of royal families. Observing intricate mourning rites was a way of advertising your upright moral character as well as your fashionability. For those in mourning—as for nuns, monks, priests, and Puritans—matte black signified renunciation, withdrawal, and social invisibility. Though the little black dress would later be synonymous with sex appeal, widows' weeds advertised that a woman was sexually experienced, but not sexually available.

While black crept back into the everyday male wardrobe in the late eighteenth century, it would take much longer for women to resume wearing black as a fashion color. Queen Victoria's decades-long bereavement for Prince Albert, who died in 1861, cemented black's association with mourning. Cheap black chemical dyes, invented in 1863, made elaborate, extended displays of grief more affordable and socially obligatory—for women, at least. Men could get away with a black armband rather than precisely prescribed gradations of head-to-toe black. Women equestrians wore black for the sake of practicality and as a nod to masculine tailoring traditions; although daring women of fashion might wear black in the evening—like the subject of John Singer Sargent's portrait *Madame X,* whose "flagrantly insufficient" black dress caused a scandal at the 1884 Paris Salon—it suggested maturity, experience, and gravitas. On a young woman, it was a statement, and not necessarily a respectable one. ("What can you expect of a girl who was allowed to wear black satin at her coming-out ball?" a character in Edith Wharton's *The Age of Innocence* asks, bemoaning Ellen Olenska's "eccentric" upbringing.) Poor and working women, too, wore black; the black dress was the unofficial uniform of shopgirls, telephone operators, and domestic servants. When Eveline Askwith, a twelve-year-old housemaid to an English vicar, wanted to be confirmed in 1903, her employer offered to buy her a new dress. "I was close to tears when the dress turned out to be a black one," she remembered;

all the other girls were wearing white, but a black dress could be repurposed on the job.[3] The classic French maid's uniform, with its black dress and starched white pinafore, is a legacy of this tradition.

But the incalculable, unprecedented losses of World War I gradually put an end to the Victorian tradition of extravagant mourning. At a time of scarcity and shortages, mourning was wasteful as well as bad for morale. "The sheer number of deaths . . . made lavish displays of bereavement seem ostentatious and inappropriate," writes fashion curator Maude Bass-Krueger. "For such large-scale societal mourning, it seemed more appropriate to mourn simply so as not to hamper the war effort."[4] Chanel's own lover, Arthur "Boy" Capel, survived the war only to die in a car accident in 1919. When Chanel said, "I shared the habits, the tastes, and the needs of those whom I dressed," that included their sorrows. As historian Lucie Whitmore has pointed out, World War I created a surfeit of young widows, who could not be expected to renounce society, work, remarriage—or, indeed, fashion.[5]

The war impacted fashion in another way: women became used to the idea of wearing a uniform. "Eight or ten months ago, a woman in a uniform was something of a novelty," *Vogue* mused in July 1918, "and, like all pioneers, she met a good deal of criticism and sarcasm." But as Paris became overrun with uniformed nurses, Red Cross and YWCA volunteers, British Wrens and Land Army girls, and American Motor Corps and Radio Corps enlistees, "the world has come to realize that the various groups of women in uniforms are serving their country as surely as the men at the front, and that these costumes have been chosen as being the most comfortable, practical, and efficient for their purpose." Military accouterments like braid, cockades, and frogging crept into civilian fashion, too. Even civilians began to dress identically: "The 'war' frock, like a uniform, is worn by everyone. To be correctly frocked nowadays, one should look like a neat lady's maid," the magazine advised, invoking a familiar domestic uniform.[6]

Even after the war, British *Vogue* noted approvingly that "no fantastic adornment attracts attention to one woman more than another. Indeed their appearance suggests that they are almost clothed in a uniform which changes in color and proves that the present generation cannot be reproached for frivolity or vanity."[7] In 1924, the magazine's American counterpart recalled:

When, during the war, a number of important and well-dressed citizens found themselves for the first time in uniform, they discovered the advantage of a costume which is appropriate to all occasions. The joys of a standardized type of dress once tried, many of them found it hard to go back to the ordinary habiliments which call for arbitrary changes so many times a day. . . . So we find ourselves five years after the war, approaching more and more surely a type of daytime dress which can be worn, with modifications of accessories, at almost any hour, from nine in the morning to six at night. This is an immense convenience for the woman of many engagements and an absolute lifesaver of the woman of limited income.[8]

The article recommended that readers invest in tailored suits for daytime but admitted that high-quality tailors were expensive and scarce. Chanel's little black dress offered an affordable solution to a long-standing problem. "Everyone was simply dressed and poor," fashion editor Carmel Snow remembered, "so Chanel began making little supple dresses of jersey. . . . She hadn't yet shortened the skirt and dropped the waistline, but I recognized even then that here was a really modern fashion for women."[9]

The time was ripe to reclaim black as a fashion color. Paul Poiret, who was known for his theatrical, Orientalist gowns in rich hues and fabrics, dubbed Chanel's work "poverty de luxe." He did not mean it as a compliment. Her restrained palette as well as her fondness for cardigans and costume jewelry elevated working-class wardrobes to the level of haute couture; her preference for utility over ornamentation was evident in her menswear-inspired styling and humble materials like jersey and tweed. Chanel told Salvador Dalí that she "took the English masculine"—that is, tailored black clothing, worn by dandies and businessmen alike—"and made it feminine." Chanel found Poiret's vivid velvets and brocades "barbaric" and "impossible," and his sultanas and odalisques mere costumes, not fashion. "Schéhérezade is easy," she said. "A little black dress is difficult." Poiret's escapist Orientalist fantasies had fired women's imaginations before the war, but in the wake of a devastating global conflict, Chanel's LBD held more appeal than harem pants and hobble skirts. "For whom, Mademoiselle, do you mourn?" Poiret is said to have asked Chanel. She replied: "For you."

Chanel was able to lay claim to popularizing the LBD because she leaned in to unrelieved black; her "Ford" didn't have a cutesy white Claudine collar and cuffs, like Premet's schoolgirl-style version, or the red outline of a dragon, like Vionnet's. It was also consistent with her stringently minimalist aesthetic. Raised in a convent orphanage, where both the children and the nuns wore uniforms of stark black and white, Chanel developed an early appreciation for austerity—and consistency. Even when she lived in an apartment at the Ritz, she slept in the maid's room, which "looked like a small, antiseptic hospital room with a narrow bed with a rosary on the brass bedstead and a crucifix over the bed. There was a table and a straight chair—little else."[10] Chanel believed that "elegance is refusal": the refusal of color, ornament, and the traditional trappings of luxury. "Fully as much as the poets," Chanel "scorns frivolity and foible," Jean Cocteau wrote in *Harper's Bazaar*. She brought black back from the realm of the dead and showed women that simplicity could be chic rather than boring.

Though Chanel's version was expensive, you didn't need to be rich to get the LBD look; indeed, the couturière welcomed people copying her design, which "lent itself to mass production as the elaborate styles that preceded her could never do," as Snow pointed out in her memoirs. "Think of the publicity it gives me," Chanel told *Harper's Bazaar* in February 1923. The many knockoffs of Chanel's "Ford" only reinforced its claims to ubiquity and utility. Just as uniforms had created a sense of camaraderie during the war, this civilian uniform allowed all women—rich and poor, old and young—to look chic, comfortable, and modern. At a time when fashion was suffering from a pronounced generational gap, Chanel's "brilliant simplicity" offered "a style that was the same for all ages and most classes."[11] (The designer herself turned forty-three in 1926.)

"Petit" means "informal" in French as well as "little," and

the LBD's unpretentiousness was as appealing as its abbreviated hemline. Chanel boasted that the little black dress used seven yards of fabric instead of the twenty that was standard for a couture piece—a fact that would not have been considered impressive or attractive before the war. If the arc of fashion bends toward informality, Chanel was ahead of the curve. She told Bettina Ballard: "I make fashions women can live in, breathe in, feel comfortable in, and look young in. You see this skirt?" She shoved her hand deep into her pockets. "It doesn't cling to me any place. I can move. I can even run quickly if I want to." A skirt you can run in, with deep pockets? Buy it in every color, but especially black.

Chanel's "Ford" changed couture as surely as the Model T changed the automotive industry, making the once-shocking little black dress a staple of women's wardrobes, one that endures to this day. Chanel's rival, avant-garde designer Elsa Schiaparelli, specialized in whimsical, wittily subversive gowns, but her "greatest fans were the ultra-smart and conservative women, wives of diplomats and bankers, millionaires and artists, who liked severe suits and plain black dresses," she admitted in her autobiography, *Shocking Life*. Even Dior—the ultimate maximalist—admired Chanel's minimalism: "With a black pullover and ten rows of pearls, she revolutionized fashion." Mary Quant, who was known for her Day-Glo dresses in the 1960s, sang the praises of black: "Of all the come-hither colors, black is the most chameleon in its sex appeal. It can be all things to all women—and all men. It can be demure as in the ubiquitous little black dress that clings with subtle suggestiveness to otherwise unsuspected curves. It can hit the height of drama in black satin." (It was a black minidress the Royal

Mail chose for Quant's commemorative stamp in 2009.) Irish novelist Edna O'Brien, writing in the fashion magazine *Mirabella* in 1994, called the little black dress "both chic and armor."

Indeed, it was (and remains) the rare garment that was as psychologically comforting as it was physically flattering and freeing. As Snow wrote in her memoir: "I remember to this day the first 'little black dress' I bought from [Chanel], of chenille with a tie belt and sleeves just over the shoulder. (I could wear it today.) I felt wonderful in it. . . . I wasn't even conscious of wearing a new dress." The timeless style is seasonless and always appropriate; as Chanel's successor Karl Lagerfeld observed, "One is never overdressed or underdressed with a little black dress." Without ever changing color, it was "a chameleon about moods and times and places," *Vogue* marveled in April 1944. Quant said it "goes anywhere and everywhere."[12] When it comes to fashion, feeling comfortable is not necessarily the opposite of feeling physically constricted; it is the opposite of feeling self-conscious, inauthentic, and unhappy.[13] Chanel's little black dress was liberating in both senses: it allowed women to be themselves, while also granting them the practicality and anonymity of a uniform.

Dior understood the power and beauty of black, but the true heir to Chanel's LBD legacy was Cristóbal Balenciaga. For the Spanish designer, black was not a color or an absence of color but an infinite range of shades and textures, from opaque to translucent, matte to glossy. It harkened back to Spain's Golden Age, when black was the rarest and most expensive dye, and severely cut garments of unrelieved black were synonymous with the political and moral authority of the Spanish monarchy. Balenciaga could make black look monastic, sculptural, or regal; minimalist or baroque. He used it for lacy baby doll dresses, sensible tailored suits, and origami-like evening gowns. Instead of unbleached muslin, he made toiles for his black garments in black percale, twill, or tarlatan, so he could gauge the effects of light and shadow on their planes and billows. "The black is so black that it hits you like a blow," *Harper's Bazaar* reported in 1938. "Thick Spanish black, almost velvety, a night without stars, which makes the ordinary black seem almost gray." Chanel—who rarely had anything nice to say about anyone—insisted that "Balenciaga alone is a couturier in the truest sense of the word. Only he is capable of cutting material, assembling a creation and sewing it by hand, the others are simply fashion designers."[14] Each of his collections included one dress that he had made entirely by himself, and it was always a black dress.

The LBD's legacy can be seen in pop culture as well as couture culture, from Betty Boop—the cartoon flapper introduced in 1930—to Robert Palmer's much-parodied "Addicted to Love" video of 1986, directed by fashion photographer Terence Donovan. When Marilyn Monroe played a flapper in *Some Like It Hot*—released in 1959 but set in 1929—she wore a series of fringed and sequined little black dresses designed by Orry-Kelly, who won an Oscar for his efforts. (Monroe's cross-dressing costar, Jack Lemmon, wore one, too.) Though the dresses were tailored to show off Monroe's famous curves and bore little relation to squared-off sheaths popularized by Chanel and her contemporaries, the color made them synonymous with the 1920s.

The slinky gowns Audrey Hepburn wore in *Breakfast at Tiffany's* certainly count as LBDs, despite their longer hemlines.

Truman Capote's novel describes Hepburn's character, the call girl Holly Golightly, wearing "a slim cool black dress, black sandals, a pearl choker." Balenciaga's protégé Hubert de Givenchy designed Hepburn's wardrobe for the film. The most

FIGURE 8. Hubert de Givenchy designed Audrey Hepburn's LBD-forward wardrobe for *Breakfast at Tiffany's* (1961). (*Paramount Pictures / Photofest*)

iconic of her LBDs is the full-length, sleeveless boatneck sheath she wears in the opening scenes. Monastically plain in front, it has a distinctive cut-out back; costume designer Edith Head altered the dress to make it even more understated, sewing up a thigh-high slit. "The little black dress is the hardest thing to realize because you must keep it simple," Givenchy explained, echoing Chanel. Paired with a multistrand pearl collar by Roger Scemama, black evening gloves, an updo, and Oliver Goldsmith's tortoiseshell sunglasses, Hepburn's LBD was instantly iconic, launching countless copies and unusually elegant Halloween costumes. Clare Waight Keller gave it a twenty-first-century update in Givenchy's Fall 2018 haute couture collection, shown shortly after Hubert de Givenchy's death. She added velvet, a hood, and pockets, but left the instantly recognizable back intact. The show closed with Hepburn's haunting rendition of "Moon River."

In 1994, a little black dress launched an unknown model-actress, Elizabeth Hurley, to fame overnight when she wore it to the London premiere of *Four Weddings and a Funeral,* starring her then-boyfriend Hugh Grant (see Plate 8). The revealing Versace gown was slit up both sides and held together by oversized gold safety pins, in a luxe update of the punk aesthetic. Versace, who knew Hurley through their mutual friend Elton John, had sent it to her fresh off the runway, without a fitting. "Liz has this intelligent face attached to that very naughty body," the designer explained. "So seeing a woman like her in this gown was a guarantee that everyone would go *pazzo* [crazy]."[15] With her daring décolleté, Hurley resembled a modern-day Madame X—but her dress caused a sensation, not a scandal.

Just a few months later and a couple of miles away, another

little black dress made an indelible impression as an instrument of royal revenge. On the evening Princess Diana's estranged husband, Prince Charles, admitted his infidelity in a televised interview, she attended a cocktail party at London's Serpentine Gallery. She had been planning to wear a borrowed Valentino dress. Instead, she chose a short, sexy LBD by Greek designer Christina Stambolian (see Plate 9). She had bought the dress three years earlier but never had the nerve to wear it. British royals rarely wear black in public, reserving it for somber occasions like funerals and Remembrance Day; short skirts, too, are verboten, especially when slit up one side and paired with a low, off-the-shoulder neckline. (Diana had never lived down the revealing strapless black Elizabeth and David Emanuel evening gown she had worn for her first public appearance with Prince Charles in 1981, an early and rare fashion faux pas.) Though not particularly daring or even unusual by the standards of contemporary commoners, the dress further emphasized Diana's break from the royal family and pushed Charles and his mistress, Camilla Parker Bowles, off the front pages the following day. The tabloids dubbed it her "Revenge Dress."

Princess Diana was a generational master of what is sometimes called "Pantone politics"—the carefully calculated use of clothing and color symbolism to sway public opinion. But the little black dress can send mixed messages. Originally an equalizing urban uniform, it quickly became associated with sexually liberated, short-skirted flappers. Even in cartoon form, it was threatening. The restrictive Motion Picture Production Code of 1934 deemed Betty Boop's little black dress *too* little and forced animators to raise its neckline and lower its hemline, hiding Boop's famous garter. Sexual innuendoes and story lines involving drug use, sexual harassment, and gambling disappeared from the cartoons, as well. The character's popularity suffered as a result, and, in 1939, the celluloid sex symbol vanished from the screen. A similar fate befell *Some Like It Hot,* which was released without the approval of the Hays Office, condemned by the Catholic Legion of Decency, and banned in Kansas for its racy content and costumes. (It became a huge hit everywhere else, though, signaling the beginning of the end for the Hays Code.) Now that it bears the weight of a hundred years of cultural baggage, the little black dress is more likely to be perceived as purposefully provocative than elegantly understated. Its very versatility opens it to criticism; just as it can be adapted for day and night, young and old, casual and formal, it's a one-size-fits-all offender. It's anything but basic.

Little black dresses have their dark side. Today, Chanel is a fashion legend, but her legacy is marred by her actions during World War II, when the Nazis occupied Paris. Chanel shut the doors of her rue Cambon headquarters and holed up in her suite at the Ritz with a German officer thirteen years her junior. After the war, she was branded as a collaborator; her business and her reputation devastated, she went into self-imposed exile in Switzerland for nearly a decade, living off her perfume sales. She staged a comeback in 1954, but few French fashion editors or clients were ready to forgive and forget. The newspaper *Le Monde* complained: "Her collection offers nothing and is a melancholy throwback to shapeless silhouettes, with no trace of bust, waist, or hips. One had the impression of flipping through a slightly yellowed old family photo album." But America was more receptive. *LIFE* magazine declared: "At seventy-one, she brings us more than a style—she has caused a veritable tempest. She has decided to return and to conquer her old position—the first." It was her successful comeback in the U.S. that put her back on top—that and the iconic Chanel suit she reintroduced in her comeback collection, which would become a daywear staple in the postwar years. "Once again," *Harper's Bazaar* fashion editor Ernestine Carter reflected in her memoir, "this extraordinary designer had created a uniform that all women would want to wear."[16]

4

THE WRAP DRESS

Working It

Charles James—the Anglo-American designer who relocated from London to New York at the outset of World War II—is best remembered for his evening gowns, sculptural creations of virtuoso technical complexity and breathtaking beauty. But he considered his most important design to be a simple black wrap dress commercially produced in 1933 as the "Taxi" dress (see Plate 10).

Late in his life, in the sexually uninhibited 1970s, James would claim that the name was derived from the fact that the dress was so easy to put on, you could do it in the back of a taxi. But that explanation, however memorable and quotable, is likely a fabrication, as was so much of James's autobiography.[1] Ads for similar wraparound dresses—called "taxicab dresses," "taxi frocks," and "jiffy-ons"—appeared in North American newspapers as early as 1922. And they were so named because they were as easy to get into and out of as a cab.

This was a notable contrast to James's intricately constructed evening gowns. "There could be a mystery as to how to get into the clothes when they arrived! Or which was the front or the back, which he might have altered at the last moment!" exclaimed his loyal client Anne Parsons, Countess of Rosse.[2] But this was no small consideration at a time when upper- and middle-class women were increasingly learning to live without a house full of servants. In 1900, domestic service was the single largest occupation in Britain; during World War I, however, most male servants enlisted, while female servants went to work in munitions factories, hospitals, and farms.

The war also affected marriage patterns; the 1921 census documented 1.75 million "surplus women" in Britain, many of whom never married due to the shortage of eligible men. Simultaneously, though, the war opened up opportunities for women to support themselves and mitigated the social stigma against remaining single. The Taxi dress offered not just ease and speed but self-sufficiency; you didn't need the help of a maid (or a husband) to get into—or out of—it. There were no corsets to lace, no tiny hooks and eyes or buttons to fasten. The facility with which the Taxi dress could be put on and taken off carried an implicit message about women's sexual availability, but its efficiency and self-sufficiency were also hallmarks of its modernity. It was not the first or last time in fashion history that practicality and charges of promiscuity would go hand in hand; the little black dress suffered the same fate (see Chapter 3).

James's high fashion interpretation of the housewife's "jiffy-on" was the precursor of Diane von Furstenberg's wrap dress and many other user-friendly dresses designed for modern living. But unlike a standard wrap dress, which is typically belted or fastened at the natural waist, James's ingenious spiral wrapped one and a half times around the body, terminating at the hip in three clasps of Bakelite, the lightweight, durable synthetic plastic patented by Belgian chemist Leo Baekeland in 1909. In 1933, James introduced a zippered version. A British *Vogue* ad touted "the latest spiral model by Charles James fitted with 'Lightning' zipp [*sic*] fastener. . . . The opening in this most original design runs spirally right round the figure." Anne, Countess of Rosse, had a zippered one made from textured black linen.

Along with Elsa Schiaparelli, James was one of the first major fashion designers to exploit the decorative possibilities of the zipper, elevating it from function to fashion. Patented in 1917, the device was first used in utilitarian clothes like military flight suits and galoshes. Early versions were called "hookless fasteners" or "slide fasteners"; the name "zipper" was trademarked by boot maker B. F. Goodrich in 1923, and quickly became genericized. "Zip" referred to the noise the metal teeth made when opened or closed, but it had long been slang for "speed." It was an onomatopoeic word mimicking the buzzing sound of an object flying through the air, much as "pew-pew" simulates gunfire.

In the 1930s, the zipper served as both a jewellike accent and a high-tech closure. Van Cleef & Arpels even designed a necklace in the form of a functioning zipper, reportedly at the suggestion of their client the Duchess of Windsor; the Zip necklace was created in 1950. The constant threat—or promise—of unzipping gave visible zippers their teeth. James would cite his "spirally constructed clothes, which assisted in launching zippers" as being among his most important and influential silhouettes.[3]

Almost as revolutionary as its nearly seamless construction and novel fastenings was the fact that the Taxi dress came in only two sizes, illustrating James's belief that a well-designed garment did not require detailed sizing. (He would issue many of his designs in two sizes, experimenting with different methods of adjusting the fit; even his trousers were cut with a diagonal waistline so they could fit three sizes at once.) Though difficult to manufacture, the Taxi dress was mass-produced and sold in department stores. In April 1934, James made a personal appearance at Marshall Field in Chicago, bringing "his spiral taxi dress," which sold for $25; they were the cheapest of his offerings, which topped out at a bridal gown at $200. He also sold "roundaround salon dresses" that followed the same spiral line.

Many years later, James claimed he'd designed his first Taxi dress for Gertrude Lawrence, the English actress who was one of his earliest clients. (Lawrence was as famous for her fashion sense as for her debts to her dressmakers; she was declared bankrupt in 1935.) Bloomsbury Group writer Mary Hutchinson was another early adopter; her friend Virginia Woolf described James's dresses as "symmetrical, diabolical, and geometrically perfect." Mathematical precision is a recurring theme in descriptions of James's work. Trained as an architect and engineer, he saw himself as a scientist and his dresses as experiments in proportion and construction. "My designs are not luxuries," he said. "They represent fashion research." He estimated that he had spent $20,000 over the years trying to perfect the cut of a sleeve. "So geometrical is Charlie James that if a stitch is crooked, the whole dress is torn to shreds," Woolf told Vita Sackville-West in a 1933 letter.

James applied his strict design principles to sculptural strapless evening gowns (see Chapter 5) as well as deceptively simple day dresses like the Taxi dress. In 1945, he installed an enormous window between his workroom and his salon, so his clients could peek behind the scenes and appreciate the intense work that kept his prices so high. Street-style photographer Bill Cunningham said: "His knowledge of anatomy, psychology, economics, technology, and aesthetics was awesome."[4] Balenciaga, the ultimate designer's designer, called James "the world's best and only dressmaker who has raised [dressmaking] from an applied art form to a pure art form." Coco Chanel and Schiaparelli paid him the highest possible compliment by wearing his dresses. But John Fairchild, publisher of *Women's Wear Daily,* did not mean it as praise when he said that for James, "fashion was an intellectual pursuit."[5] Indeed, James's obsessive perfectionism was a financial liability; he rarely made a profit and died destitute in 1978, holed up in seedy rooms at the Chelsea Hotel, still tinkering with dresses he'd designed in the 1930s.

By the early 1940s, the spiral line had lost its dizzying allure; instead, wrap dresses had become synonymous with maternity wear, nursing uniforms, and "Hoover aprons," shapeless coveralls designed for doing housework. It took a woman—designer Claire McCardell—to appreciate its fashion potential as well as its practicality (see Chapter 1). In 1942, McCardell debuted the "Pop-Over" dress, which could go from cleaning to cocktails.

"You just pop it over something nicer underneath when doing the housework," one fashion editor explained.[6] This "household device de-luxe" was ideal for women whose servants had gone into war work, leaving them to cope with chores alone. It illustrated a *Harper's Bazaar* roundup of housekeeping tips

FIGURE 9. Claire McCardell's patented "Pop-Over" dress with its matching oven mitt appeared in a Lord & Taylor advertisement in *Harper's Bazaar* in May 1943. (*Harper's Bazaar, May 1943*)

under the headline "I'm doing my own work—and what's more, I'm doing it well." Made in sturdy, washable denim, the Pop-Over came equipped with a coordinating pot holder, housed in a roomy pocket. With a price tag of just $6.95, it was "so becoming you can greet your guests in it," the ads read.

McCardell sold more than 75,000 of the dresses in its first season and included a version of it in every subsequent collection. The patented Pop-Over remained on the market for years, outlasting the war to become a dress in its own right rather than a cover-up.

After World War II, American designers established themselves as sportswear specialists. (For formal gowns and cocktail dresses, most women still looked to Paris, or authorized copies of French couture.) Female designers like Tina Leser (who won a Coty Award in 1945 for her "wrapped skirt silhouette," among other innovations) and Bonnie Cashin (who was inspired by the Japanese kimono) offered "wraparound" skirts, dresses, and even blouses. Advertisements for these styles stressed their convenience, touting features like big pockets and drip-dry fabrics. The wrap dress was "versatile," "convenient for warm weather," "a four season favorite," and "something a woman can throw on in a hurry and still look her best." It "flatters every figure." It was both "crease-resistant" and "easy to iron because it opens out flat." All these features made it ideal "for a busy woman's life."

Often designed with minimal seams and no fiddly buttonholes or zippers, wrapped styles were as easy to sew as they were easy to wear, and pattern companies made do-it-yourself wraps accessible to the masses. These patterns could be adapted to make halter-neck styles and long-sleeved, short-sleeved, or sleeveless versions. And they weren't just for housework or housewives anymore. In addition to being a seasonless style, the wrap dress was increasingly advertised as a round-the-clock style "for casual or dressy wear" that a woman could wear "from morning 'til night," for cleaning or cocktails. "Fashion has taken a liking to the wraparound idea," Mary Hampton, the fashion editor of *The Fresno Bee*, noted in 1944. "When fashion likes an idea it can do miracles to embellish it." (However, she added that it wasn't for everyone: "If you are the flat-chested type either skip it or add chiffon to your bra.") James would revive his spiral line in 1950, creating his most successful dinner dress ever: a figure-hugging, bias-cut dress in ruby-red silk faille with an asymmetrical wired collar and a wraparound skirt, constructed without side seams or darts. *Vogue* nailed the appeal of this elegant wrapped silhouette when it featured it in the November issue, noting that it "looks like a different dress from every angle."

Vicky Tiel began wearing her own wrap skirts and dresses as a fashion student at Parsons in the early 1960s. But her casual, uncomplicated designs didn't impress the male faculty, which included James Galanos and Norman Norell, known for their couture-quality ready-to-wear. One day, she walked into class wearing a turquoise burlap wrap skirt and found her classmate Mia Fonssagrives wearing a similar skirt in purple. "Our skirts have to meet," Tiel recalled saying in her autobiography. The two went into business together, launching a fashion line in Paris, where their leather and crochet miniskirts were a hit with the yé-yé girls, an emerging youth counterculture.

But no designer, male or female, has become more synonymous with the wrap dress than Diane von Furstenberg. Her wrap dress, created on her dining table in 1973, was greeted as a symbol of the feminist movement. "To some, the wrap became a manifesto for the liberated woman of the 1970s," as von

FIGURE 10. Diane von Furstenberg modeling her iconic wrap dress, which she called "a manifesto for the liberated woman of the 1970s." (*Adc / Shutterstock.com*)

Furstenberg put it. "The dress fit in with the woman's revolution by allowing the millions of women going off to work to be well dressed and out the door in a minute without worrying about wrinkles, buttons, zippers, hooks and eyes. The wrap also fit in with the sexual revolution; a woman who chose to could be out of it in less than a minute." Von Furstenberg believed that "women wanted a fashion option besides hippie clothes, bell-bottoms, and stiff pantsuits that hid their femininity."[7] In addition to the wrap dress, she sold "little sexy dresses" in other styles—notably shirtdresses—as well as separates, including pants. But it was the wrap dress that resonated with women's lib. At a time when women's pants were finally gaining widespread acceptance, the fashion sensation of the 1970s was a dress.

Offered in a rainbow of prints, von Furstenberg's "little bourgeois dress" seemed to fulfill all the promises of the wrap dress ads of the 1940s and 1950s at once; it was, as the designer often said, "flattering, feminine, and, above all, functional." It was worn by Gloria Steinem and First Lady Betty Ford. One hangs in the Smithsonian. It landed von Furstenberg, just twenty-nine, on the cover of *Newsweek* in 1976; she was the first fashion designer to receive that honor. (In her cover photo, she wore one of her shirtdresses rather than a wrap dress. "I preferred the shirtdress and rarely wore the wrap myself," she confessed in one of her two autobiographies.) Bill Blass called her "the designer who put dresses back on women."[8] In an era of yo-yo hemlines, the wrap came in one demure length, landing just below the knee. The V-neckline highlighted the bust. The wide sash minimized the waist. And the A-line skirt completed the hourglass shape. The skirt was full enough to walk in, but clingy enough to accentuate curves. Its adjustable ties meant it could fit and flatter a variety of figures. The soft cotton-rayon jersey was comfortable, breathable, and machine-washable (although von Furstenberg quietly updated the label to read DRY CLEAN ONLY after the dyes in some of the prints ran). It was stretchy enough that it didn't require ironing. It cost $86—a steep step up from McCardell's Pop-Over, though the similarities between the two were not lost on *New York Times* fashion writer Bernadine Morris, who called the wrap "a housedress, dressed up in nice fabric."[9] It was a price working women were willing and able to pay, however, especially for a dress that could do double duty, going from daytime to dinner. At the height of the style's popularity, von Furstenberg sold 25,000 wrap dresses per *week,* easily eclipsing the success of Halston's Ultrasuede shirtdress, the must-have trend of 1972. While Halston's dress held a similar easy-care, easy-to-wear appeal, its silhouette and fabric were less forgiving and less conventionally feminine.

It helped, too, that von Furstenberg was a real-life princess and a bold-faced name in gossip columns (one *Newsweek* head-line read: "Rags & Riches"). Born in Brussels, von Furstenberg had an economics degree from the University of Geneva and spoke five languages fluently, but she had no fashion industry experience; she couldn't even sew. Her celebrity friends and nightclub antics provided invaluable publicity. Actresses like Dina Merrill, Cheryl Tiegs, and Candice Bergen wore her wrap dresses; Cybill Shepherd wore one in *Taxi Driver.* But the wrap dress didn't need any borrowed glory; it flew off the racks on its own merits. "It is a lesson to some of the great designers that you don't have to keep coming out with something new," said

Vogue editor Diana Vreeland, an early champion of von Furstenberg's work. "Do one thing very, very well." As Halston pointed out, "if her name were Diane Schmaltz, it would have worked, too."[10]

The appearance of von Furstenberg's wrap dress coincided with the peak of the second wave of the feminist movement, which focused on workplace equality. The Equal Rights Amendment—first proposed in 1923—had been reintroduced in Congress in 1971, with a ratification deadline of 1979. Contentious public debates over the ERA formed the backdrop to the rise (and fall) of the wrap dress. In 1960, 38 percent of American women worked outside the home; by 1980, more than half did. They were increasingly moving into white-collar jobs and positions of power. And they needed something to wear. "Fashion then was either very far-out hippie or drip-dry polyester," von Furstenberg told the Associated Press in 1998. "There was nothing in between."

In *The Woman's Dress for Success Book* (1977)—one of several similar titles promoting "power dressing" published in the 1970s—John T. Molloy offered advice on how women in the workplace could "promote success, express authority, and attract men" through their clothing. "There is one firm and dramatic step women can take toward professional equality with men," he wrote. "They can adopt a business uniform." Molloy didn't mean a wrap dress but a two-piece, tailored skirt suit worn with a high-necked blouse, accessorized with heels and an attaché case. (Even in the revised 1996 edition of the book, Molloy bluntly stated: "If you want to wear pants to the office, don't wear pants to the office.") Molloy's books were based on statistical data and market research, not fashion trends or personal opinion; while the definition of appropriate workplace attire has changed, much of his advice (like "dress for the job you want") is still valid today.

The wrap dress gave women an alternative "business uniform." Unlike a suit, it could go from the office to a restaurant or nightclub. It didn't need to be dry-cleaned. And, thanks to Vogue Patterns, you could "Do-Diane-Yourself" for as little as $13. The message of von Furstenberg's ads—"Feel like a woman, wear a dress!"—was a powerful one at a time when both feminists and their foes were navigating rapidly shifting gender identities. Just as many men felt threatened by women adopting masculine roles and garments, many women feared that espousing feminism meant denying their femininity. In von Furstenberg's wrap dress, you could "feel like a woman" even if you were succeeding in a man's world.

When von Furstenberg started her company, "people were convinced feminists were ugly," Steinem said. The *Ms.* magazine cofounder delighted in proving them wrong; she had famously, convincingly posed as a Playboy Bunny for a *Show* magazine exposé. Von Furstenberg agreed. Being a feminist didn't mean "you have to look like a truck driver."[11] Nevertheless, she had a hard time convincing the male-dominated garment industry to take a chance on her. As *Vogue* explained, "women were into pants. Sexy dresses were out." The wrap dress was undeniably sexy. Von Furstenberg encouraged this perception, framing it as an expression of women's sexual agency rather than their sexual vulnerability. As she was fond of saying: "If you're trying to slip out without waking a sleeping man, zips are a nightmare." She constantly reminded journalists and customers how easy it was to get into *and* out of the wrap dress. "Simplicity and sexiness," she told *Vogue*. "That's what people want."[12] She gave women permission to look (and feel) sexy all day, not just after dark. Her first wrap dress was in a green-and-white wood-grain print, but more predatory prints, like snakeskin and leopard, soon followed.

The "wrap dress" moniker "took a while to catch on"; initially, it was called "the wraparound dress" or even "the Diane dress."[13] Von Furstenberg's first wraps were tops and skirts, not dresses. "The top was inspired by the ones ballerinas wear over their tutus," she told *Los Angeles Magazine* in 2014. "I knew I wanted to make a simple little dress that would flatter a woman's body, so I combined the wrap and skirt." She also looked beyond ballerinas to more ancient models. "It's actually a very traditional form of clothing. It's like a toga, it's like a kimono, without buttons, without a zipper. What made my wrap dresses different is that they were made out of jersey and they sculpted the body."[14] The American fitness boom was just hitting its stride; while von Furstenberg's clinging clothes didn't exactly "sculpt" the body, they showed off gym-sculpted physiques to the best advantage (see Chapter 10).

Newsweek called von Furstenberg "the most marketable designer since Coco Chanel"; menswear designer John Weitz agreed, telling the *New York Amsterdam News* that "Diane may end up as the Chanel of the age because her clothes make sense." Like Chanel's little black dress, the wrap dress was all things to all women, regardless of age, body type, or social class (see Chapter 3). And, like Chanel, von Furstenberg was her own best advertisement, literally appearing in her own ads as well as the covers of fashion magazines and pattern catalogs. Despite her royal title and jet-setting lifestyle, her customers felt a connection with her as a working woman and a working mother. "She knows her customer," Oscar de la Renta said. "She understands women and the power of femininity."[15]

In July of 1976—the year von Furstenberg sold $64 million worth of her jersey wrap dresses worldwide—*Vogue* asked her if people might get tired of them. "They're so easy to wear," von Furstenberg replied. "People don't get tired of blue jeans, do they?" The wrap dress was equally versatile, practical, and timeless. Nevertheless, von Furstenberg stopped producing it in the late 1970s due to market saturation, from both her own dresses and cheap knockoffs. She moved into licensing, putting her famous name on cosmetics, fragrances, and luggage. When bankruptcy forced her to sell her company in 1983, she returned to designing. She brought back the wrap dress, relatively unchanged and with the same $86 price tag. But, like many of her licensed products, it sacrificed quality for quantity, and ended up in discount stores rather than department stores.

Meanwhile, von Furstenberg was preoccupied with the small, pricey "couture" boutique she opened in New York in 1985—a business plan at odds with her image of accessible, affordable glamour. And the designer herself had changed: she was no longer a jet-setting twentysomething princess but a divorced, working mother of two. ("I gave up the princess title so I could use the Ms. title," von Furstenberg quipped.[16]) The couture business failed; instead, the Seventh Avenue success story of 1985 was a collection by another female designer, Donna Karan. Her "Seven Easy Pieces"—usually consisting of a black bodysuit, wrap skirt, jacket, cashmere sweater, trousers, tights, and white shirt, sometimes augmented by a dress, a scarf, or "something leather"—was the original capsule wardrobe. As versatile as the wrap dress was, working women wanted something even more flexible to take them from day to night: chic mix-and-match separates.

In January 1985, *Vogue* published the proceedings of a fashion "symposium" of prominent designers, politicians, and businesswomen titled: "Is Fashion Working for Women?" The year 1984 had been a banner one for working women: Geraldine Ferraro ran for vice president, and more than half of American women held jobs, including three hundred on corporate boards of directors. More women were earning their own money, and, more importantly, paying for their own clothes. The article pushed back against John Molloy's vision of a uniform of gray flannel blazers and flats, unpopular with men and women alike. Carol Phillips, the president of Clinique, quipped: "I think men *are* comfortable when they see a woman in a little business suit. They know that she's already intimidated." Morgan Stanley VP Brenda Landry agreed: "Many men don't want women *at* work!" The question of what women should wear to the office was just another form of gatekeeping, one shifting goalpost among many.

Yet it could not be ignored. "We can all deny it and say the only thing that matters is the issues, but that's not really the case," San Francisco mayor Dianne Feinstein told *Vogue*. "Women are still new to positions of power, and therefore people tend to make snap judgments about them. . . . People tend to be very critical of women's clothing." The words "appropriate" and "masculine" and "comfortable" came up frequently in the discussion. "Psychologically, for women to adopt men's clothing was like a promotion," designer Gianfranco Ferré reflected. "But I don't think that kind of promotion was a necessary one. . . . If a woman has a dress that suits her, it is almost easier to wear a dress than anything else."[17]

Diane von Furstenberg came to the same conclusion. She reacquired the license to the wrap dress and relaunched it again in the fall of 1997, after noticing that young women were wearing vintage wrap dresses they'd bought in thrift stores, riding a wave of disco-era nostalgia. This time, she reined in the original wide collar and replaced the cotton-rayon jersey with more luxurious silk jersey. The hemline was higher, and so was the price tag: $200. Von Furstenberg took out ads in *Interview, Vanity Fair,* and *The New York Times Magazine* showing a laughing model in a wrap dress with wild 1970s curls and dark lipstick. But instead of the you-go-girl slogan "Feel like a woman, wear a dress," the tagline addressed the twenty-three-year-old elephant in the room. It read: "He stared at me all night. Then he said . . . 'Something about you reminds me of my mother.'"

5

THE STRAPLESS DRESS

Women on the Brink

Style, sex, and science converge in the strapless dress. Its exact origins are a matter of debate; though the term "strapless" was used in the late 1920s, it usually indicated a halter or off-the-shoulder neckline rather than a true strapless dress. Once hemlines began to climb, designers started looking for new areas of women's bodies to bare, experimenting with plunging necklines, one-shouldered gowns, and backless styles as well as bare arms and bias-cutting. As hemlines dropped back down for formalwear in the early 1930s, a fashion magazine joked: "In the evening, you can show everything except ankles."[1]

After a decade of the boyish "garçonne" look, women were ready to flaunt their curves again; the new fashions accentuated the waist and the bust, using the bias cut to mold fabric to the natural shape of the female body (see Chapter 1). Strapless costumes were among the suggestive styles seen in Hollywood films before the Motion Picture Production Code was instituted in 1934 (see Chapter 10). Actress Libby Holman wore one on-stage in the Broadway revue *Three's a Crowd* as early as 1930. But *Vogue*, the fashion bible, gave the credit for popularizing the strapless dress among civilians to Paris couturier Main-bocher.

"Away with shoulder straps—decrees Mainbocher," the magazine announced in July 1934. "Whalebone sewed strategically into the bodice removes all cause for alarm." By "whalebone," *Vogue* meant not bone but baleen, the hairy, flexible keratin plates that take the place of teeth in some whales—or, more likely, a man-made approximation of it. (Christian Dior was still using real baleen in the 1950s, but many other couturiers substituted "boning" made from plant fibers, processed feather quills, or thin strips or spirals of steel.) Baleen was the backbone of fashion before the Industrial Revolution, when it was used to stiffen hoop petticoats and corsets. Strong but flexible, it was history's plastic. You could heat it and shape it, or split it into long, narrow shafts, which were stitched between layers of fabric. It was increasingly replaced by steel in the late nineteenth century, and plastics in the twentieth. But the term "whalebone" continued to be used as a metonym for corsetry; though not actually made of bone, whalebone and its substitutes acted as bones, surrounding and supporting the flesh like an external rib cage. In strapless styles, though, their job was to support the bodice, not the body. "Just as an engineer when building on shifting soil uses pile construction, so wise dressmakers use whalebone to bolster bodices," *LIFE* magazine explained in January 1938. "As an added precaution, elastic at great tension (the suspension-bridge principle) is frequently used to hold top of the dress firmly above bust line."

FIGURE 11. In 1934, *Vogue* gave Mainbocher credit for inventing the strapless gown, also called the "naked dress" at the time. (*René Bouët-Williaumez, Vogue, ©Condé Nast*)

Strapless gowns were marvels of engineering. They "seem to stay in place only by a miracle," *New York World-Telegram* fashion editor Gertrude Bailey marveled from Mainbocher's atelier. When actress Pert Kelton "introduced the strapless evening gown to Hollywood" by wearing one to the Cocoa-nut Grove in the summer of 1934, it made headlines in New York: "Strapless Gown in Movie Town Won't Slip Down," the *Daily News* rhymed. These early strapless gowns were cut in pronounced peaks above each breast, almost as if the moor-ings of a spaghetti-strap gown had simply been snipped. And they were revealing not just in front but in back, where they dipped even lower. Mainbocher's spring collection instantly became the talk of two continents. "Mainbocher has a most significant collection this mid-season," Canada's *Windsor Star* reported. "Buyers . . . favor his sensational backless and strap-less evening bodices, which are boned in front to insure mod-esty." Even his famously flat-chested client Wallis Simpson could wear them.

By the fall, Mainbocher had abandoned bare shoulders for flesh-toned tulle shoulder straps. But for the media and the pub-lic, it took much longer for the fantasy and novelty of the strap-less gown—or "naked dress," as it was sometimes called—to wear off. In April 1937, *LIFE* reported, strapless gowns accounted for one-third of all formal gown sales in America. Fashion jour-nalists were full of advice on how to wear the risky new style gracefully. As the 1938 winter party season approached, one headline declared: "Shoulders Must Have Beauty in Strapless Gown." The style demanded "a beautiful, graceful throat, and shoulders that are smooth, white, and perfectly rounded. If you intend to have a strapless dance dress, by all means begin now to improve the texture of your skin on the neck and shoulders, fill out hollows, and learn to carry your head like a queen." The article recommended swimming the breaststroke to tone the shoulders and pectoral muscles, "which support the breasts," but cautioned women to avoid bathing-suit tan lines "or else do a complete bleaching job."[2] (Strapless bathing suits reinforced with steel cups facilitated strap-free tanning.) Other suggestions included scrubbing one's elbows "twice a day," bleaching them with fresh lemon juice, and using foundation and powder on the shoulders and arms.

Fashion magazines began to feature hairstyles designed for going strapless—swept up and off the face in front. A strapless gown was ideal for showing off a dramatic necklace, but women with short necks were discouraged from wearing them. Florists puzzled over how to attach a corsage to a strapless gown, and the wrist corsage was born. Perfect posture was essential; neither the shoulders nor the spine should slouch. A perfect fit was crucial, too. "Strapless dresses are expensive because each one must be fitted to the wearer's torso," *LIFE* explained; for that reason, they were status symbols as well as sex symbols. Even a custom-fitted strapless dress was hard to pull off with an unusually large—or small—chest. According to columnist Rhea Talley of the Louisville *Courier-Journal*: "The acid test for straplessness is this: does the onlooker pay too much attention to the actual mechanics of keeping it on? Then wear straps." Women with large upper arms were advised to avoid the style altogether.

Just as important as what strapless dresses displayed was what they hid. The strapless style prompted a flurry of innovation in undergarments. While bandeau bras were already on the market, they were useless because they flattened the very contours needed to support the bodice. The new strapless, backless, plunging bras were marketed as "evening brassieres." As early as 1936, women could buy three-way convertible bras "whose satin straps can be adjusted to be worn for daytime, with a halter . . . or entirely removed for a strapless evening gown. . . . It is one of those trick garments which actually works."[3] *New York Times* fashion critic Bernadine Morris described the Merry Widow—a bustier inspired by the costumes Lana Turner wore in the 1952 movie musical of the same name, based on Franz Lehár's 1905 operetta—as "a super-bra, that extended past the waist, nipping it firmly, covered the top of the hips, and had long garters to attach to the stockings." The garment's long line offered more support than a bra, even in a dress with a low back. These high-tech foundations (plus some low-tech tricks, like medical adhesive tape) "enabled women of assorted ages and shapes to look like slim-waisted, high-bosomed, bare-shouldered shepherdesses in strapless evening gowns," *LIFE* claimed in July 1938.

Despite these shortcuts, it is perhaps not surprising that Hollywood starlets—with pinup physiques and makeup artists on call—were the first to wear strapless dresses, given the challenges of wearing them well. But the style quickly became associated with another group blessed with physical advantages and sartorial daring: teenage girls. Indeed, the history of the strapless dress belongs to these young women more than sexy screen sirens. While the Rita Hayworths, Gina Lollobrigidas, and Marilyn Monroes of the world vamped in curve-hugging, gravity-defying sheaths, debutantes and prom queens waltzed in shoulder-baring strapless gowns with full, feminine skirts and delicate floral decorations in pure white or pretty pastels. "Surprisingly enough, a strapless white gown, by its suggestion of innocence, is most devastating of all," observed New York *Sun* fashion editor Kay Thomas in May 1938.

Mainbocher may have pioneered the strapless gown, but seventeen-year-old debutante Brenda Frazier deserves credit for making it an eveningwear staple when she appeared on the cover of the November 14, 1938, issue of *LIFE* in a strapless gown of pale pink velvet. The occasion was New York's Velvet Ball, the first major party of the 1938 social season, held in the grand ballroom of the Waldorf-Astoria Hotel on October 28. The annual charity fundraiser doubled as a publicity event for the Velvet Guild, a garment industry trade organization. Naturally, all the debs wore velvet, and the female guests received party favors donated by Schiaparelli: velvet heart necklaces bearing perfume bottles. Frazier, the chair of the Debutante Committee, had planned to attend in a rosewood velvet dress with a sweetheart neckline and short, shirred sleeves, but changed her mind and went strapless at the last minute. All the debs wore full skirts; a Broadway director had choreographed a "Hoopskirt Waltz" for the occasion. The sold-out event netted $12,000 for charity, but "as the traditional object of a debutante party, the presenting of eligible young men to marriageable daughters, it was probably a failure," *LIFE* admitted. "The pace of New York life is such that most young men in active business have no time for deb parties. The college boys and recent graduates who make up present-day stag lines are for the most part out of work." As a fashion moment, however, it was an unqualified success.

Debutante balls functioned as symbolic weddings, initiating

young women into the marriage market while also advertising their social and sexual desirability. The strapless gown—almost always white for one's formal debut, though pastels were acceptable for other parties—advertised both physical maturity and the moral purity befitting a bride; its long, full skirt was

FIGURE 12. Debutante Brenda Frazier was photographed in a strapless gown of pale pink velvet for the cover of *LIFE* in 1938. (*Getty Images*)

demure, yet also practical for the waltzes, cotillions, and other formal dances debs performed at balls. Strapless gowns made their first blushing curtsies during the 1936 and 1937 debutante seasons; however, Frazier's name became synonymous with the style just as it was reaching its peak popularity. In addition to appearing on the cover of America's most popular magazine sans straps, Frazier had posed for the July 1938 issue of *Harper's Bazaar* in a strapless white gown. She attended the September opening of the El Morocco nightclub wearing what New York *Daily News* society columnist Nancy Randolph called "one of those how-dya-keep-it-up creations—a strapless gown of black taffeta." In October, she sported a strapless gown of black velvet and sky-blue satin at Mrs. Vincent Astor's party for the Musicians' Emergency Fund. At the Tuxedo Ball the same month, "practically every debutante who was present wore a crinoline—a great, wide, billowing one, with an hourglass waist and strapless décolleté. Loveliest of the Loveliest was Brenda Frazier . . . the 'glamour girl' of the current season."[4] In November, Frazier was spotted dancing at the Rainbow Room in strapless white satin. The same month, she posed for *Vogue* in a strapless black velvet gown and attended a friend's coming-out ball at the Waldorf-Astoria's Starlight Roof—a penthouse supper club with a retractable roof—in "a strapless, bouffant dress of shell pink velvet." The low neckline showed off "a diamond necklace outshining every other present with the exception of Mrs. William Randolph Hearst's," syndicated society columnist Inez Robb reported, adding: "Debutantes in diamonds are something new on the social scene this year."

Though Frazier would not make her own formal debut until December, she had already been dubbed the "deb of the season" by the media; gossip columnist Walter Winchell coined the term "celebutante" to describe her, a neologism later applied to Paris Hilton. "The modern New York debutante has become as well publicized and commercialized as a fan dancer or a new hairdo, and for good reason," the *LIFE* cover story explained. While the deb circuit had once been limited to the ultra-wealthy—the proverbial "400" who could fit in Mrs. Astor's ballroom—"the post-Depression debutante is presented not only to her family's intimate friends nor to New York's plutocracy, but to the general public—to the profit and delight of charity organizers, national advertisers, and department-store executives." The doors of high society still remained closed to outsiders, but, for the first time, they could watch through the windows, aided by the ravenous media.

And high society wasn't what it had been in Mrs. Astor's day. Frazier may have gone to the right schools—Chapin and Miss Porter's—but she came from new money rather than old. The Bergen *Evening Record* joked that "though not the richest" debutante, "she's most generously endowed of the year"—a comment paired with a suggestive photo of Frazier in a strapless gown, taken from an overhead angle, at the October opening of the Iridium Room nightclub. (Her date was tactfully cropped out). As far as New York's plutocracy was concerned, Frazier's genius for publicity was further proof of her outsider status. That only made her more attractive to the adoring masses. Society columnist Cholly Knickerbocker pronounced: "She belongs to the public created for her just as much as if she were a 'movie' star, or an operatic diva." At the end of her debut season, on December 29, "a jury of glamour experts" named Frazier one of eleven "glamour kings and queens of

1938," alongside such luminaries as the Duke of Windsor, Hedy Lamarr, Orson Welles, and Bette Davis, the United Press reported. Gossip columnist Elsa Maxwell, one of the judges, declared: "She has made the American debutante the most attractive young woman alive."

The strapless dress was a fitting symbol for this new breed of celebrity socialite, whose seemingly miraculous poise and physical perfection was perpetually laid bare for public consumption. And the debutante was, in turn, an unimpeachable fashion role model for young women, who were desperately in need of one. The term "teen-ager" was already being used in fashion marketing, but it was usually accompanied by illustrations of models with girlish faces and figures in childish floral frocks—more tween than teen. There was no middle ground between that group and the increasingly important "college" demographic. Women enrolled in college in unprecedented numbers in the 1930s, though often with the goal of becoming better wives and mothers rather than expanding their career prospects. *Mademoiselle,* founded in 1935, targeted college students and recent graduates between the ages of eighteen and thirty-four and originally aspired to be a literary magazine as much as a fashion magazine. Frazier's fame put a sweet-but-sophisticated face to the burgeoning teenage retail demographic. "Clothes for Teen-Age Girls Have the Chic of a Debutante," read the headline to a November 1938 story by Associated Press fashion editor Adelaide Kerr. "That problem child—the teenage girl . . . is not a fashion orphan any more" but "a person in her own right," Kerr wrote.

Famous for being famous, Frazier parlayed her celebrity into a modeling career, a fling with Howard Hughes, and a

Hollywood screen test. A perfume was created for her; the comic strip *Brenda Starr* was named after her. She married—then divorced—a fellow celebrity, former pro football player John "Shipwreck" Kelly. Later in life, she battled eating disorders and depression and came to regret her early notoriety, reflecting ruefully on 1938: "I was a fad that year—the way midget golf was once a fad, or flagpole sitting."[5] Or, indeed, strapless dresses.

The strapless craze came to a premature end thanks to World War II. The wide-shouldered, military-inspired look prevailed. Fabric for long, full skirts was scarce; so was metal for the boning required to support strapless dresses. It wasn't until after the war that fashion rediscovered the silhouette and sales surged, with a boost from Rita Hayworth. In the 1946 film *Gilda*, Hayworth sang—and danced—in a strapless black satin Jean Louis sheath inspired by John Singer Sargent's portrait *Madame X* (see Chapter 3). Hayworth paired the gown with long black satin gloves that ended right at the neckline, visually extending the expanse of shoulder and bosom on display. The gown's formfitting skirt, slit to the thigh, bared even more. When Hayworth threw her arms over her head without losing her top, she gave women everywhere the confidence to unstrap. (Her red hair and femme fatale frock would provide inspiration for another iconic strapless siren, cartoon chanteuse Jessica Rabbit.) Two months after the film's Valentine's Day premiere, Epsie Kinard of the Newspaper Enterprise Association syndicate reported that "both Paris and Hollywood have succumbed to the allure of almost topless dresses which bare the shoulders, back, and part of the bosom. . . . What the bodices of these dresses lack—which is a lot—the skirts more

FIGURE 13. Rita Hayworth gave the strapless style a postwar boost in *Gilda* (1946). (*Ned Scott / Columbia Pictures / Photofest*)

than make up for with yards of drifting net, layers of tulle, lavish embroidery, tuftings of feathers, and peplums of plumes."

Costume designer William Travilla borrowed Hayworth's trick with the gloves when he dressed Marilyn Monroe in a hot pink satin strapless gown to sing "Diamonds Are a Girl's Best Friend" in 1953's *Gentlemen Prefer Blondes*. But the Technicolor hue ensured that there could be no confusion between the two iconic looks. Travilla lined the satin gown with stiff felt to help it keep its shape; an enormous bow on the backside exaggerated Monroe's every bump and shimmy. In Federico Fellini's *La Dolce Vita* (1960), Anita Ekberg cavorted in Rome's Trevi Fountain wearing a gravity-defying strapless black velvet dress by Italian designer Fernanda Gattinoni; the mermaid moment inspired countless homages and advertisements, including a Peroni beer commercial.

But there was another side to the strapless revival of the 1950s that called back to the style's high-society origins. With a demure décolletage and a cotillion-worthy full skirt, the style appeared youthful and ladylike—especially when rendered in virginal white, like the gold-embroidered Givenchy gown Audrey Hepburn wore in 1954's *Sabrina,* or the woven chiffon gown Grace Kelly wore in 1955's *To Catch a Thief,* designed by Edith Head. Kelly's costume was designed to show off the diamond necklace at the heart of the heist plot. "There had to be enough fabric showing in the tight shot so that the audience knew [she had clothes on]," Head remembered in her memoirs. "Now this may sound simple, but it wasn't."

Strapless didn't always mean sexy, then; depending on the shape, color, and styling, it could be tame enough for princesses, politicians' wives, and brides. Argentinian First Lady

Eva Perón wore a strapless white tulle Christian Dior gown to a gala at the Teatro Colón in Buenos Aires in 1951—a real dress resurrected as an iconic stage costume in Andrew Lloyd Webber's musical *Evita*. In the same year, Princess Soraya of Iran chose a strapless silver-and-white Dior gown and matching jacket for her wedding to Shah Mohammad Reza Pahlavi. The first American First Lady to veto straps was Mamie Eisenhower, who bought a strapless Jacques Heim gown of "creamy Chantilly lace reembroidered on a foundation of black net" with "an immense foaming skirt" in May 1952 in Paris, where her husband served as the NATO commander before his presidential run.[6] The Associated Press called the fashion-conscious First Lady "that rare phenomenon, a grandmother who looks wonderful in a strapless dress"; the style was already beginning to be perceived as a fashion for the young.

Princess Margaret made headlines when she became the first member of the British royal family to wear a strapless gown in public in May 1951, at a London concert. Even as other prominent women embraced the style, it was a controversial choice for a princess, and it "would have spun prim Queen Victoria into a shocking faint," as the International News Service put it. When Dior made his first gown for Margaret—a strapless tulle confection with a large satin bow at the back—he thoughtfully "sent it with tiny tulle straps which could be added to the dress at will" and "a tulle fichu to shroud the shoulders."[7] (The gown was her favorite; she wore it on her twenty-first birthday.) And when Margaret wore a strapless pink satin gown and stole to a ball in Jamaica during her Royal Tour of the Caribbean in 1955, the *Woman's Sunday Mirror* criticized her persistent penchant for low necklines. But at the November 1965 White House dinner for the princess, hostess Lady Bird Johnson wore a strapless gown, and the most talked-about outfit of the evening belonged to a different guest, Mrs. Henry Ford II, who wore a "low-cut strapless white sheath—so low that she occasionally gave a feminine hike to the bodice but on one occasion did it too late," the *Washington Star*'s syndicated society columnist Betty Beale reported.

Charles James, who was born in England and dressed the British elite from his Mayfair atelier, relocated his fashion business to America at the start of World War II. He had trained as an architect and engineer, and he approached dressmaking as both science and seduction (see Chapter 4). "There is no greater master than James at building bodices," *Vogue* testified. The strapless dress was the ultimate exercise in "fashion engineering," as James called it. His 1938 "Umbrella" dress was the first strapless gown with a separate strapless underbodice—a foundation of stiffened grosgrain.[8] His strapless chiffon "Swan" gown of 1951 required thirty layers of fabric and nearly one hundred pattern pieces. But his masterpiece was the strapless satin and velvet "Clover Leaf" ball gown Austine Hearst commissioned for President Eisenhower's 1953 inaugural ball, with its cantilevered quatrefoil skirt. Due to the gown's technical complexity—and James's inveterate perfectionism—it was not ready in time for the inauguration in January; Hearst wore it to Queen Elizabeth II's coronation ball in June instead.

Weighing nearly fifteen pounds, the Clover Leaf stayed on thanks to its internal scaffolding of materials James had used during his brief career as a milliner: featherboning, nylon mesh, buckram, and horsehair braid. A separate underbodice kept the torso perfectly positioned; an undulating waistline distributed the weight of the vast, stiffened skirt evenly over the hip bones. The bodice curved up slightly under the arms before dipping in back; James even customized his dress forms, indenting the underarm to follow the natural line of the rib cage, so his dresses wouldn't bunch under the arms.[9] His cerebral approach to the strapless dress stripped it of Hollywood-style sex appeal and elevated it to sculpture; his dresses were so rigid that they could stand up even without a body in them.

But James's custom-made, precision-engineered gowns were too rare—and expensive—to have a widespread impact on fashion. Once again, the strapless trend was fueled by a debutante: Angela Vickers, played by seventeen-year-old Elizabeth Taylor in the film *A Place in the Sun*. For the pivotal coming-out party scene in which Taylor's character meets leading man Montgomery Clift, "the dress had to be white and important," costume designer Edith Head said. It also had to stand the test of time: though Head completed the costumes in early 1949, the film wouldn't be released until the summer of 1951, in order to avoid competing with 1950's *Sunset Boulevard* for audiences and awards. She deliberately focused on the silhouette, giving the costumes very few details so they wouldn't date quickly. This strategy had the added benefit of showcasing Taylor's "flawless" figure, with a nineteen-inch waist and breasts Richard Burton would famously describe as "apocalyptic."[10]

Head was inspired by the slim waists and full skirts of Dior's New Look of 1947, which she believed "would be around long enough for me safely to dress Elizabeth in full skirts" (see Chapter 6). It was a look popular with actual debutantes: at Chicago's Débutante Cotillion and Christmas Ball of 1949, sponsor Marshall Field awarded a strapless Dior gown of 118 yards of

FIGURE 14. Elizabeth Taylor wore a much-copied strapless gown designed by Edith Head to play a debutante in *A Place in the Sun* (1951). (*Paramount Pictures / Photofest*)

white satin and tulle to the debutante who brought in the most donations to the fundraiser.[11] For Taylor, Head conjured up a white tulle gown with three-dimensional white velvet violets sprouting from the sweetheart neckline. "It's very difficult to look dated with flowers," she noted. "The flowers made the bust look fuller. The combination of the full bust and wide skirt accentuated the waist, making it appear even smaller than it was." Taylor's cropped hairstyle left her shoulders bare; she wore no necklace, gloves, or wrap, as she did in other party scenes. "Do I make you nervous?" Taylor asks Clift. "Yes," he answers, on behalf of every man in the audience.

The debutante circuit had slowed to a halt during World War II. As more women entered the workforce and the armed services, debutantes were increasingly viewed as frivolous; most of their escorts had enlisted, anyway. But the tradition came back with a vengeance in the 1950s, as a war-torn nation found solace and stability in the social ritual, which was no longer confined to the cosmopolitan elites but expanded to middle-class suburbs across the country, with similar (but separate) events exploding in Black communities.[12] These new debutantes tended to juggle their social lives and charity work with college classes, and they came out at organized cotillions rather than private balls. And they did it wearing strapless gowns.

Taylor's gown became one of the most copied dresses in Hollywood history. Although she wears other strapless gowns in the film, the distinctive violets—and the crackling sexual tension of the scene—made it iconic. It was instantly knocked off by eveningwear manufacturers and "mass-produced to hang in every department store in the country." Head—who won her third Oscar for the film—recalled: "One of my young friends reported a party she attended at the time of the picture's release; in attendance were *seventeen* 'Elizabeth Taylors' decked in white violets." You didn't need Taylor's natural assets to wear the style, thanks to "waspies"—waist-cinching corsets that created a wasplike hourglass silhouette—and push-up bras. (Though not new, underwire bras became cheaper and more comfortable after the war; in 1955, the "Wonderbra" was trademarked in the U.S.) If velvet violets weren't available, ruffles and ruchings of chiffon and lace could camouflage flat chests. London designer Janey Ironside, who dressed debutantes of the early 1950s for their balls and presentations at Buckingham Palace, remembered in her autobiography that "eighty percent of the ball dresses were ordered with tight, strapless bodices and immensely full, long skirts. The top layer, usually of organza or some light fabric, and the three (at least) layers of net underneath were gathered until the waistband could accommodate no more. . . . Storing them was a problem. . . . We could not turn round for these enormous white puff balls."[13] Ironside blamed the trend on Dior's influence, and the full, long skirts certainly bore his imprint. But it was Elizabeth Taylor (and Brenda Frazier before her) who made strapless synonymous with debutantes.

A Place in the Sun marked Taylor's transition from a child star to "Paramount's gorgeous teenager," as she was billed. She seemed to carry a whole generation with her. The term "teenager"—barely used before the 1950s—was suddenly on everyone's lips. "They are responsible for so many of our purchases," *Cosmopolitan* marveled in November 1957. "They inspire so many designs and styles and institute so many fads, that it is possible to regard them as a vast, determined band of blue-jeaned storm troopers, forcing us all to do exactly as they dictate."[14] The adolescent "bobby-soxers" of the 1940s now constituted a marketing force to be reckoned with. Postwar prosperity gave them spending power; increased car ownership gave them mobility and independence. "Teenagers of today have more freedom than their parents did, and consequently more choices to make," the *St. Louis Globe-Democrat* explained in May of 1951. "Industry recognizes them as people, designing special fashions for them; numerous books and magazines are published for their special entertainment and enlightenment." Instead of dressing like children, their mothers, or their college-aged sisters, teenage girls developed a taste and style unique to their in-between age group, one chronicled by a new crop of teen-focused magazines like *Seventeen, Miss America, Junior Bazaar,* and *Deb,* short for "debutante."

A high school prom was the closest most teenagers of the 1950s would ever get to a debutante ball; it was a democratized version of the symbolic entry into the marriage market, which emerged along with compulsory high school attendance in the United States in the first half of the twentieth century.[15] For many teens, it was the first time they wore formal dress, slow-danced, or rode in a limousine; many proms crowned a "king" and "queen," lending an element of competition to the fashion show. Usually held in the spring, the prom marked an end as well as a beginning, as the senior class celebrated its imminent graduation. The strapless dress, long associated with debutantes, became the go-to for high school promgoers in the 1950s; in it, "the 'ugly duckling,' the gangling teenager, can be turned into a swan," *The New York Times* prophesied.[16] Taylor herself wore her Edith Head gown as a prom dress: as a publicity stunt, Paramount awarded a UCLA student a "date" with Taylor to a "prom" on the studio lot.

But the same style that was admired and applauded on a wealthy socialite like Brenda Frazier or an elegant ingenue like Elizabeth Taylor was likely to be attacked as offensive or inappropriate on a suburban teenager, especially if she had a less-than-perfect figure. Showing too much skin was incompatible with Christian ideals of modesty dating back to the Garden of Eden. Catholics protested against the "immodest" style. Mormons condemned it, too: in a 1951 speech at Brigham Young University, Elder Spencer W. Kimball criticized "immodest dresses that are worn by our young women," singling out strapless styles. One student in the audience, sophomore Bertha Clark, had already purchased a strapless dress for an upcoming school formal. She remembered: "My dress was beautiful, but it wasn't 'kimballized,' so I bought a little jacket I could wear with it. Most of my friends 'kimballized' their wardrobes."[17] In 1954, American Army wives and daughters in Germany were banned from wearing strapless dresses on base. Further controversies erupted as the style became popular for quinceañeras and bat mitzvahs: coming-of-age celebrations for even younger girls, which included a religious ceremony.

A high schooler wrote to Emily Post complaining that her mother felt she was too young to wear one to a dance. "I can't see what difference a little strap makes across the shoulder," she protested. The syndicated etiquette columnist replied: "Having personally lived through fifty years of changing fashions, the strapless dress is, in my opinion, the most destroying to beauty of any that has gone before. A towel pinned around the chest never has been considered a beautifying line." Tellingly, Post sidestepped the question of whether strapless gowns were age-appropriate, condemning them as merely unflattering. But, along with other teenage vices like makeup, smoking, hot rods, and rock and roll music, they sparked contentious debates over how grown-up teenagers were supposed to be.

For teen girls, wearing a strapless dress was a rite of passage as exciting as buying a training bra, and for the same reason: it meant that they finally had breasts. Maybe those breasts weren't as apocalyptic as Elizabeth Taylor's, but they had arrived, and nothing announced their presence more effectively or dramatically than a dress seemingly held up by nothing but soft tissue. Though boys might wear their first tie or tuxedo to a school dance, these fashion statements were less indicative of physical maturity and individual taste. The strapless dress was the apotheosis of the female body, fashion, and identity. An advertisement for Gorham flatware that appeared in *American Girl* magazine in 1956 depicted a teenage girl in a strapless gown gazing into a mirror decorated with wallet-sized photos of teenage boys. The tagline read: "When does a girl grow up?"[18] At a time when many women—Taylor and fellow teen idol Natalie Wood included—married and settled down before they turned twenty, it was a pertinent question. While many women had put off marrying during the war, the average age of brides dipped in the 1950s. Was a teen girl a child in a grown-up body, or a woman on the brink of adulthood and marriage? Teenagers—and everyone around them—had theories but no answers. The frothy strapless party dress embodied this precarious balance between innocence and experience.

Appropriately, wedding gowns began to go strapless, too, though brides usually added a matching jacket for the religious ceremony. In August 1951, Emily Post strongly discouraged these antics in her syndicated etiquette column, saying "a dress that is so much as collarless is out of place in church. . . . The very idea of straplessness is as unthinkable as that of a bridegroom in shorts!" Though civil ceremonies became more common during the Depression, most marriages were still performed in churches and synagogues where hats and gloves were the norm, not bare shoulders and cleavage. The pastor of the West Oxford Baptist Church in North Carolina resigned when his congregation voted to permit a wedding with bridesmaids in strapless gowns to take place in 1953. Fans of the style argued that strapless wedding and bridesmaid gowns were practical because they could be worn again as eveningwear. But the opposition persisted. In 1961, syndicated advice columnist Ann Landers declared: "A bride should not be wearing a strapless gown. The traditional bridal gown has long sleeves (summer and winter)." In May 1964, Post still had not relented: "A bride in a strapless dress would be in very bad taste." It would take a generation (and *Vogue* editor–turned–bridal designer Vera Wang) to convince etiquette mavens to say yes to the strapless wedding dress. As ceremonies became increasingly secular—and fashion forward—in the 1990s, it became hard to find a wedding gown that *wasn't* strapless. But even then brides were recommended to cover up with a stole or shrug if they married in a church or synagogue.

A wedding was responsible for a lawsuit involving two

THE STRAPLESS DRESS 121

strapless dresses. In 1953, the Associated Press reported that a London dressmaker had sued Irene Bonstein and Mavis Mercado, who had not paid her for their strapless bridesmaid gowns. The clients countersued, contending that the ill-fitting gowns caused them "mental distress" because the unlined bodices caused chafing, and they could not take part in the dancing at the reception. After a fashion show in his private chambers, Judge Wilfrid Clothier (really) ruled that Bonstein and Mercado had to pay for the gowns, saying: "It must seem to anyone that such support is precarious. It is meant to attract men, and a lady who selects such a dress must be prepared to put up with a considerable amount of discomfort. She must even be prepared to support the bodice by hand, if necessary."[19]

Perhaps hastened by mishaps such as these, the strapless dress met its "demise" in the late 1950s. But it returned on a wave of nostalgia in the fall of 1965, along with ankle-strap shoes. "I'm tired of covered skin," designer James Galanos confessed to *The New York Times* in August. Instead of wasp-waisted, full-skirted ball gowns in the New Look mode, however, the new strapless dresses were "high-bosomed, sirenish columns that flow straight to the floor without emphasizing the waistline." As First Lady, Jacqueline Kennedy frequently wore strapless styles to state dinners and on foreign tours. Bra manufacturers scrambled to accommodate the slim silhouette with boneless bandeau bras. "Women don't want to go back to the Merry Widow look," one told *The Times*.[20]

The 1970s saw another revival of the strapless style, as part of a wider trend for body-conscious designs. Made in light-weight fabrics, they could be held up by a band of elastic rather than elaborate boning. By the 1980s, the strapless look even crept into daywear, though usually with a matching jacket; however, many schools and workplaces immediately banned these new styles.

Even now, in the heyday of "naked dresses" (see Chapter 7), straplessness can still cause a scandal—especially when teenagers are involved. In 2013, the Board of Education of Readington, New Jersey, upheld a middle school principal's decision to ban strapless dresses from an eighth-grade dance, fearing that they "could fall off," risking "the possibility of the dissemination of such an occurrence through social media." Although the board agreed to allow clear straps and single straps, parents protested that the dress code was "arbitrary and sexist," especially after the (female) principal declared the dresses "too distracting for boys," regardless of whether they led to cyberbullying.[21] Of course, it was not the dresses that were "distracting," but the bodies in them; once again, the dress stood in for its wearer, and the dress code preemptively penalized the "distracting" girls rather than the "distracted" boys.

In the twenty-first century, the clavicle has become "the unlikely object of erotic interest and social taboo," argues fashion historian and legal scholar Richard Thompson Ford. Schools continue to punish girls for wearing clothes with straps and collars that expose the collarbone, as well as strapless styles. Miniskirts, leggings, and tight jeans are also frequent targets of school dress codes, which overwhelmingly impact girls. "Many of the expressed rationales for high school dress codes assume female bodies are inherently distracting," Ford writes. "When high schools enforce overly strict, discriminatory dress codes, they're doing what schools know how to do best: they are *teaching* their students. . . . They are teaching them by example to identify bad girls by what they wear and to treat those girls badly."[22] As a result, sexist dress codes extend to the adult world, where they are found in airplanes, restaurants, and workplaces. Like strapless dresses themselves, it's a mystery how they stay in place.

6

THE BAR SUIT

Reinventing the Postwar Woman

On the bitterly cold morning of February 12, 1947, the fashion press, retail buyers, celebrities (including Rita Hayworth), aristocrats, ambassadresses, and even royalty packed into the small, airless salons of Christian Dior's Avenue Montaigne couture house for a show that would make fashion history.

Word of mouth had aroused "a fever of popular curiosity." Unable to afford a publicity campaign, Dior had worked on the collection—his first—in total secrecy, trusting gossip to do the rest. The fledgling couturier may have been an unknown quantity, but he had one thing the more established couture houses who had weathered the war did not: an elegant maison newly decorated in a serene faux–Louis XVI style, chosen to provide a neutral backdrop to the clothes. The paint was barely dry on the white and pearl-gray walls; the carpet had just been installed that morning; "the last bang of the hammer was actually heard as the first visitor entered."[1]

Vogue editor Bettina Ballard "couldn't get near the door because the pushing crowd was so intense," she remembered. Once she finally made her way inside, where it was so crowded that spectators were jostling for space on the staircase, the excitement was palpable: "I was conscious of an electric tension that I had never before felt in the couture. People who were not yet seated waved their cards in a frenzy of fear that something might cheat them of their rights. Suddenly all the confusion subsided, everyone was seated, and there was a moment of hush that made my skin prickle."[2]

"Défilé de mode"—the French term for "fashion show"—is literally translated as a fashion parade or fashion procession, and that's a more accurate description of what transpired in Dior's crowded salons than the kind of theatrical runway presentation we would recognize as a fashion show today. "Mannequins," as fashion models were then called, moved slowly through the maison, occasionally twirling, never smiling. They navigated a gauntlet of fashion editors and buyers perched on gilt chairs or armchairs. (As at the court of Versailles, "there was a world of hierarchical difference between" those seated in chairs and those granted armchairs, *Harper's Bazaar* fashion editor Ernestine Carter noted.[3]) There was no music; a barker (*aboyeuse*) called out the name and number of each "model"—meaning dress—as it entered the room, in English as well as French.

Dior's *défilé* was livelier and more theatrical than a traditional couture show, as the mannequins' "graceful pirouetting walk founded a new fashion in modeling," the designer remembered.[4] Carter, who was in the audience, remembered it differently, describing "the model girls arrogantly swinging their vast skirts." The first mannequin's skirt swung so furiously that it toppled the tall ashtrays dotting the grand salon. "All round the salon you could see the English tugging at their skirts trying to inch them over their knees," Carter quipped. "The models swirled on contemptuously, bowling over ashtrays like ninepins."[5] As more mannequins waltzed by, "all at the same exciting tempo, the audience knew that Dior had created a new look," Ballard reported. "We were witnesses to a revolution in fashion and to a revolution in showing fashion as well."[6] Susan Alsop, an American in the audience, wrote to a friend back home in the States: "It is impossible to exaggerate the prettiness of 'The New Look.' . . . Gone the stern padded shoulders, *in* are soft rounded shoulders without padding, nipped-in waists, wide, wide skirts about four inches below the knee."[7] Some of these skirts were pleated, scalloped, or ruffled, using as much as eighty yards of fabric.[8] There were ninety looks in total, all variations on the same hourglass silhouette with soft, rounded shoulders and long, sweeping skirts.

At the end of the show, the audience erupted in applause, and Dior came out to take his bow. "As long as I live, whatever triumphs I win, nothing will ever exceed my feelings at that supreme moment," he later remembered.[9] He wasn't the only one feeling giddy. "Even after all these years of seeing clothes beyond count, nothing has ever come up to the exhilaration of those first Dior collections," Carter reflected.[10] Afterward, some of the jaded fashion journalists in the audience "stayed and tried on the extraordinary new clothes, slightly punch-drunk with the excitement of it all, whirling around in the knife-pleated skirts," Ballard confessed.[11]

It was not Ballard but *Harper's Bazaar* editor Carmel Snow who coined the term "New Look." ("It's quite a revolution, dear

Christian! Your dresses have such a new look!") Significantly, it was not the "Dior Look," although everyone knew who was behind it; it was a whole new way of dressing that all women could achieve, even without a couture budget. And it was a look that war-weary women were eager to emulate, not one that they felt had been dictated to them by an imperious (male) designer. "It was because women longed to look like women again that they adopted the New Look," Snow would insist in her memoirs. "The change was due to a universal change of feeling, of atmosphere. Fashions, I believe, aren't *put over* on women." Carter offered a more straightforward explanation: "Never has so universally becoming a fashion nor one so enduring been devised. Tall women, short women, large women and small women, older women, young women, the New Look suited them all."[12]

Of course, the New Look was actually a revival of an old look. Dior had spent years designing for the houses of Robert Piguet and Lucien Lelong before his career was interrupted by World War II and a stint in the army. In November 1941, on the brink of war, *Harper's Bazaar* had shown skirts falling well below the knee, advising its readers: "Watch this skirt length. If your first impulse is to cut it shorter, you're in a rut. If it looks right to you . . . you're a woman of the future." After a decade of wartime clothing rationing and restrictions on fabric-wasting details like pockets, pleats, and ruffles—still in effect in much of Europe—Dior's collection simply picked up where fashion had left off. "After so many years of wandering, *couture* . . . wanted to revert to its true function, of clothing women and enhancing their beauty," Dior reflected. "It was time for fashion to forsake adventure and make a temporary return to base." Women who had grown accustomed to Rosie the Riveter coveralls, utility garments, hand-me-downs, and mannish military uniforms "still looked and dressed like Amazons," Dior complained. "But I designed clothes for flowerlike women, with rounded shoulders, full feminine busts, and hand-span waists above enormous spreading skirts. . . . I molded my dresses to the curves of the female body, so that they called attention to its shape. I emphasized the width of the hips, and gave the bust its true prominence."[13]

Few women had naturally full busts and handspan waists; some of Dior's own mannequins wore falsies to give their busts "true prominence." While bras had largely replaced corsets during World War II—to conserve materials as much as for the comfort of women employed in war work—the New Look revived them. As Dior famously declared: "There can be no fashion without foundation." He had once hoped to become an architect, and he boasted that his dresses were "constructed like buildings, molded to the curves of the female form, stylizing its shape."[14] Audience member Susan Alsop praised him for putting "such well-made armor inside the dress that one doesn't need underclothes; a tight bodice keeps bust and waist small as small, then a crinoline-like underskirt of tulle, stiffened, keeps the skirt to the ballet skirt tutu effect that Monsieur Dior wants to set off the tiny waist." The designer lined almost all of his skirts with cambric or taffeta, to help them spread—a technique abandoned even before wartime fabric restrictions. By enforcing a uniform silhouette, Dior leveled the playing field. Ballard said it was his "inner construction that made the Dior shape prevail whatever the shape of the woman, thus giving fashion assurance to women all over the world. . . . The day was passing when a few smart women influenced the fashion world by the way they wore clothes. Dior spread the happy thought that every woman in a Dior dress, or even a copy of a Dior dress, was a figure of fashion."

"Have you heard about the New Look?" Nancy Mitford wrote from Paris, in a letter to her sister Diana in England. "You pad your hips & squeeze your waist & skirts are to the ankle it is bliss." The many layers also kept the wearer warm, an important consideration to someone raised in drafty country houses; not only did the padding act as insulation, but "now one will be able to have knickers over the knee." Like its poofy predecessors the farthingale, the hoop petticoat, and the crinoline, the New Look skirt proclaimed one's wealth—fabric was expensive, after all—while also offering physical comfort. Just as those earlier understructures untangled women's legs from layers of petticoats, Dior offered freedom from the narrow, knee-length sheaths of wartime skirts, their dimensions dictated by governments, not fashion trends. The New Look gave women a reason to buy entirely new wardrobes, and thus revitalized the Paris couture industry, which had become a shell of itself during the Occupation. The media frenzy surrounding Dior's landmark collection announced to the world that French fashion was back in business.

Though the "Corolle" collection consisted of ninety similarly silhouetted outfits—modeled by just six mannequins—the Bar Suit is the one that has lodged in our collective memory and become synonymous with the New Look. It's the suit Dior Barbie wears; it's on the covers of countless Dior books and exhibition catalogs. Why? It wasn't a bestseller; it barely cracked the top ten highest-selling dresses of the collection, probably

FIGURE 15. Christian Dior's Bar Suit—with its pleated jersey skirt and jacket "hip padded like a tea cozy"—was featured in the April 1, 1947, issue of *Vogue*. (*Serge Balkin, Vogue, ©Condé Nast*)

because its structural complexity made it both expensive and difficult for the licensed copyists who made up much of couture's clientele to knock off.

The much-reproduced Willy Maywald photograph of Dior's model Renée Breton wearing the Bar Suit is one reason for its fame. (Dior wrote that "of all my mannequins, Renée is probably the one who comes nearest to my ideal."[15]) But the suit in the photo isn't the 1947 Bar Suit; Breton didn't even work for Dior at the time of his debut show. Instead, it's a reproduction Dior made in 1955 for a lecture at the Sorbonne; the jacket lacks the shawl collar, six buttons, and closed front of the original. However, the photo bears testament to the iconic status the Bar Suit had already achieved in just a few years.

The suit's dramatic black-and-white palette—precisely fitted on top, padded and pleated at the bottom—is another reason for its iconic status. The jacket alone required four yards of ivory silk shantung; the wool skirt—long and, even more decadently, knife-pleated at a time when fabric was still scarce—unfurled like a corolla, the petals of a flower. (Dior had a love of gardening dating to his childhood in Normandy.) The instantly recognizable Bar Suit was widely copied and replicated; Dior and his successors referenced it, more or less literally, in almost every subsequent collection. As recently as 2011, Junya Watanabe paid homage to it, transforming the jacket into a black leather motorcycle jacket, paired with a fluted black polyurethane skirt (see Plate 11).

But the suit's name offers the strongest clue to its celebrity. The Bar Suit was named for the bar at the Hotel Plaza Athénée—a stone's throw from Dior's headquarters on the Avenue Montaigne—which the couturier frequented. Inspired by the chic women who frequented the bar—a word that came into English from the French, not the other way around—it was particularly designed for drinking cocktails. The concept of the cocktail emerged during Prohibition, as a way to make bootleg liquor more palatable by mixing it with syrups and sodas. But cocktail dresses were largely a postwar phenomenon. Dior described them as "elaborate and dressy afternoon frocks," preferably in black; since cocktails were usually consumed standing up, the dresses often had bows, stiff petticoats, and other features that would have made sitting difficult. Dior even defended his profligate use of fabric to the United Press syndicate by explaining that cocktails required dresses distinct from office and streetwear.

This category of clothing was so new that it sometimes ran afoul of formal dress codes. *Vogue* editor Bettina Ballard remembered wearing a calf-length black satin evening ensemble Dior had designed for Lelong in 1946 to London's 400 Club "with terrific pride . . . only to be turned away at the door as not being in evening dress. Englishwomen swept by me in their trailing prewar chiffons, shedding beads as they walked, but in my new Paris creation for the evening I was considered underdressed." The incident made headlines on both sides of the Atlantic, with newspapers (and *Time* magazine) debating whether "short skirts" should be allowed in nightclubs. The Bar Suit, then, was emblematic not just of the return of celebration and socializing after the war but of women's newfound freedom to enjoy it. It changed not only the look of women's fashion but how the world looked *at* women.

While Dior had designed his collection for "an established clientèle of experienced buyers and habitually elegant women," he was pleasantly surprised to find that young women (including actress Dominique Blanchar and bohemian singer Juliette Gréco) wanted to wear it, too. "His timing had been perfect," Ballard wrote. "The fashion world needed a name to grasp, a line to follow, someone who could restore a glow to fashion." The New Look was just the thing to wear to the balls and parties and performances that seemed to take place every night now that the war was over. "It was as if Europe had tired of dropping bombs and now wanted to let off a few fireworks," Dior quipped. And it wasn't just Europe. In March 1948, *LIFE* profiled Dior and declared: "Women all over the Western world sit sewing in skirt facings, removing shoulder pads and feeding their families on spaghetti to save enough money to buy a new spring outfit."[16]

Not everyone thought it was a good look, given the ongoing recovery efforts. A Dior photo shoot in Montmartre was interrupted by a spontaneous protest as women ripped a decadent Dior dress from the model's back. In America, the "Little Below the Knee Club"—an organization that claimed 300,000 members nationwide—campaigned against the New Look (with slogans like "It shows everything you want to hide, and hides everything you want to show" and "Mr. Dior, we abhor dresses to the floor"), only to admit defeat around the time of the style's first anniversary in February 1948. A proposed Canadian counterpart, the Society for the Prevention of Longer Skirts for Women, attracted widespread support. One surprising holdout was the Duchess of Windsor, the former Wallis Simpson. In October 1947, the mainstay of the Best Dressed List told the United Press: "I have not changed the length of my skirt and what is more I do not intend to." Perhaps she felt some loyalty to the United Kingdom, her husband's homeland, where clothing was still being rationed; alternatively, she may have agreed with those Parisiennes who considered the longer hemlines unflattering and unsexy.

Rationing didn't stop Princess Margaret from embracing the New Look. Being younger and further down the line of succession, she could get away with being more fashion-forward (and French) than her sister, Princess Elizabeth. Shortly after Dior's debut, Margaret began wearing long, full skirts with nipped-in waists. In 1949, she set out for her first continental tour, visiting Italy, Switzerland, and Paris. In between sightseeing stops in the French capital, she found time to visit several couturiers, including Jean Dessès, Jacques Fath, Molyneux, and Christian Dior, where she acquired a strapless ball gown, which she later remembered as her "favorite dress of all. . . . It was my first Dior dress, white strapless tulle and a vast satin bow at the back. Underneath the huge skirt there was a kind of beehive, fixed like a farthingale. It meant I could move any way, even walk backwards, without tripping up."[17] She wore a different Dior—a one-shouldered organza gown from 1950's "Oblique" collection—to her twenty-first birthday party in 1951, as well as in the Cecil Beaton portrait taken to mark the occasion. In 1952, she represented the royal family at Dior's landmark fashion show to benefit the Red Cross at Blenheim Palace in Oxfordshire. She would remain a loyal Dior customer until her death.

Dior described Margaret as "a real fairy-tale princess, delicate, graceful, exquisite" who was "keenly interested in fashion."[18] But it was another fairy-tale princess who came to embody the New Look to his American audience: Cinderella. Walt Disney began production on his animated retelling of the

Perrault fairy tale in 1948. When the film premiered in 1950, its debt to the New Look was lost on no one, least of all Dior himself. "Now that *Cinderella's fairy godmother* no longer exists, the *couturier* must be the magician," he wrote in his 1956 autobiography, *Dior by Dior*.

Disney once confessed that his favorite moment in animation history was "when Cinderella got her ball gown." Everyone loves a rags-to-riches tale, and Cinderella is the ultimate makeover movie; Disney didn't hand his heroine a ball gown so much as magically refashion her on-screen from head to toe. In 1950, though, Cinderella symbolized not only a cosmetic transformation but a cultural one. The entire movie can be read as a parable of postwar consumerism, with Dior himself as the fairy godmother. The Axis Powers of wicked stepmother and ugly stepsisters are vanquished and humiliated. Underemployed farm animals benefit from a sudden jobs boom, and victory garden pumpkins become slick new rides. What better metaphor for the fragile path back to peace and prosperity than a glass slipper?

Disney's sole previous animated fairy-tale heroine, Snow White, had the rosy cheeks and cropped hair of an all-American girl of the 1930s. And she was very much a girl: a flat-chested Kewpie doll who was cute rather than beautiful. While the ideal adult body is proportionally eight heads high, Snow White was only five heads high—childishly top-heavy even by cartoon standards. Her appearance was inspired by nineteenth-century storybook illustrations, and she wore the same Renaissance-style gown for most of the film. But the New Look introduced a new feminine ideal. When Dior described his "flowerlike women," he could have been talking about Cinderella.

No Disney film is more wardrobe-driven than *Cinderella*, and most of the plot elements involving clothing were added by Disney, fueling criticism that the studio turned a classic fairy tale into a bourgeois, capitalist fantasy. Indeed, virtually every plot twist centers on Cinderella's clothes. At the outset of the film, Cinderella—orphaned and forced into a kind of domestic slavery by her stepmother, Lady Tremaine—appears in a straight, knee-length skirt that perfectly conforms to the Utility Clothing Scheme, Britain's restrictive wartime style specifications. As her fortunes continue to plummet, her clothes become more tattered and patched. She adds a torn apron and a headscarf—a staple of female fashion during World War II, when hat-making materials were in short supply and many women went to work in factories, where uncovered hair was a safety hazard.

When Prince Charming throws a ball, Lady Tremaine tells Cinderella that she may attend—*if* she is properly dressed. Friendly mice (a Disney innovation) make do and mend, updating an old pink gown with a repurposed sash and beads discarded by Cinderella's stepsisters. With its full, puffed sleeves and girlish bows and flounces, the gown resembles a prewar hand-me-down; Cinderella even wears a Snow White–style bow atop her loose hair. But her jealous stepsisters, encouraged by their mother, rip the dress to shreds. As they depart for the ball, Cinderella's fairy godmother appears and conjures up a gown so beautiful that not even the mice recognize the heroine. Her tragically tattered and outmoded wardrobe makes Cinderella's magical transformation to a New Look debutante all the more dramatic. Her icy silver ball gown has a full skirt with a gathered overskirt that evokes both the polonaise style of the eighteenth century and the Bar Suit's peplum jacket. Her shoulder-length, pin-curled 1940s hairstyle becomes 1950s bangs and a sophisticated updo anchored by a headband, with nary a bow in sight. She accessorizes with earrings, a choker, and long white gloves.

To finish off the ensemble, the fairy godmother replaces Cinderella's sensible black ballet flats (popularized by designer Claire McCardell during the war, when leather was scarce) with a pair of deliciously impractical glass slippers (standing in for postwar pumps). But when she accidentally stays out past midnight, her dress reverts to rags. Miraculously, the glass slippers are preserved; Prince Charming finds one on the palace steps and, because the slipper will not fit anyone but Cinderella, uses it to find her. But Lady Tremaine breaks the slipper before Cinderella can try it on; so transformed is she that even the smitten prince can't be certain it's her until she produces the matching slipper and proves her identity. Audiences of 1950 dreamed of not just postwar recovery but complete transformation: throwing off the tattered remnants of the past and diving headfirst into a world of long-denied comfort and beauty. Cinderella's extreme makeover from ration-book fashion to couture chic reenacts the deprivations of World War II and its Dior-designed happily ever after.

Even in America—where clothing was never rationed the way food and fuel were—the New Look was welcomed as a return to the luxury and elegance of the 1930s, as if the war hadn't intervened at all. American women may have worked in factories and knitted for victory, but they were also encouraged to dress well, have traditional white weddings, and wear elaborate makeup and hairstyles to boost morale as well as the domestic economy. "Your legs and feet must look their infinite best," *Vogue* advised in 1944. "If sheer stockings are scarce—try a leg makeup with an emollient against chapping. . . . Sandals make a pedicure essential." It is hardly surprising, then, that American women didn't greet the New Look with the same raptures as Nancy Mitford and her compatriots; they had been less deprived of fashion and beauty. But the New Look certainly influenced American fashion, as did Disney's hugely popular film, even inspiring a line of *Cinderella*-branded bridal wear.

The New Look inspired another unlikely American classic: the poodle skirt. While often dismissed as a kitschy trend, the statement skirt of the 1950s domesticated and democratized the New Look, transforming it so completely that its French connections have been largely forgotten today. The complex history of this iconic style—now standard sartorial shorthand for an entire decade in movies, television shows, and Halloween costumes—belies both its innate provincialism and its vanishingly short life span. Like many fashion fads, the poodle skirt's origins were manifold; it was born of long-simmering stateside stereotypes of French fashion culture, combined with excitement over the new textiles and full-skirted silhouettes coming out of postwar Paris.

Long before Dior came on the scene, "poodle" was an American metonym for "French," with all the sophistication and stylishness that implied. Though the poodle wasn't a French breed, the dogs were often called "French poodles," because trained poodles were a long-standing feature of the French court and circus tradition. (The animals' elaborate haircuts, too, may have suggested a typically French strain of arrogant chic.)

From the mid-1930s, poodles appeared on printed textiles along with other animal-inspired motifs as the popularity of florals waned. By 1945, Americans could purchase "French poodle print" dresses and lingerie as well as poodle-themed home décor, including painted ceramic tiles, ashtrays, and wallpaper. In 1947, a Missouri newspaper, the *St. Joseph News-Press,* asked: "Why don't you have a suit or coat in the new shade of poodle gray, a lovely blue-gray tone that is characteristic of French poodles?" At the same time, live poodles invaded American homes; they went from being the twenty-fifth most popular dog breed in the country in 1946 to number one in 1960. Stars like Tyrone Power, Elizabeth Taylor, Katharine Hepburn, Claudette Colbert, Joan Crawford, Sandra Dee, and Elvis posed for fan magazines with their photogenic and on-trend pets.

The French were in on the joke. Dior himself designed a gold poodle brooch; poodle aficionado Grace Kelly owned several Cartier poodle brooches. In 1951, Pierre Balmain sent a lilac-tinted poodle down his runway, carried by a model in a matching coat. This much-publicized moment became a meme of its time; it was subsequently referenced in the 1952 film *April in Paris,* in which Broadway chorus girl Doris Day represents American theater at a French art exposition, and 1957's *Funny Face,* set in the Paris fashion world, as well as many magazine layouts. In 1955, Joan Collins posed in her pink bedroom with her dyed-to-match poodle, her hair styled in the short, curly "poodle cut" (or "poodle clip") that first became popular in 1951. The new 'do had appeared on the January 1952 cover of *LIFE* magazine, which reported that one New York salon "poodles nearly 500 heads a day" and noted that the style was "approved by clothes designers as a balance to current full skirts, small waists, and high necklines." The poodle skirt and the poodle cut went hand in hand, or paw in paw.

But the "poodle" in "poodle skirt" initially referred to its fabric, not its French-inspired cut or canine appliqué. "Poodle cloth"—or *poilu* (meaning "hairy") in French—was a stiff, fuzzy textile used for slippers, coats, and mittens as well as skirts. A 1953 ad for the May Department Store of Boston, for example, depicted a "virgin wooly poodle suit" with a pencil skirt. Other "poodle skirts" had the flaring silhouette but no dog or other design; these skirts were just as likely to be described as "pinwheel skirts."

Vincent Monte-Sano, Jr., of the Monte-Sano coat company, claimed credit for introducing poodle cloth to the U.S. market in 1949. "We introduced coats in that very nubby fabric at that time and named the fabric poodle cloth," he told the United Press in 1951. The textile was eventually adopted for "coats, suits, dresses, and even hats" as well as skirts. Poodle cloth resembled industrial carpeting more than dog fur. However, it was soft and, most importantly, bulky enough to hold its shape, without being too heavy or requiring twenty (or more) yards of fabric per skirt. This precise combination of lightness and stiffness made it ideal for bringing the New Look to the mass market. By 1949, Dior himself had moved away from long, full skirts, but he brought the hourglass silhouette back in 1951, and couturiers Jacques Fath, Jean Dessès, and Paquin followed suit. "After several seasons of straight skirts, it was inevitable that fullness should return," Fath explained to the Australian newspaper *The Age*, introducing his pyramidal "Arrow" line of spring 1951. This time, the American fashion industry was ready.

FIGURE 16. Three women model poodle skirts at Toronto's Ryerson Institute (now Ryerson University) in 1956. (*City of Toronto Archives*)

The poodle skirt as we know it—a long, full skirt bearing an image of a poodle—wasn't widely worn until the summer of 1952. California singer-turned-designer Juli Lynne Charlot claimed to have invented it years earlier, in 1948, when she made a simple, Dior-inspired circle skirt out of felt and decorated it with sparkly appliquéd Christmas trees for a Hollywood holiday party. Charlot chose felt because it came in pieces wide enough to cut into a circle; she didn't know how to sew. But the stiff, fuzzy, lightweight textile had the same texture as poodle cloth and held its shape in the same way. Charlot sold similar skirts with different designs—including an Eisenhower campaign skirt—at Los Angeles department stores, using the skirt's excess fabric as a canvas for the appliquéd motifs. In 1952, she created a pattern for a skirt with a poodle on it; this may have been the same "poodle skirt" sewing pattern released by the Carol Curtis company that year. Newspaper ads emphasized: "You get both in this pattern—the full skirt and the poodles! The popular dog figure is done in appliqué . . . felt, poodle cloth, contrasting linen, or cotton," embroidered with anatomical details. Of course, by this time, full skirts and circle skirts made of "poodle cloth" were nothing new; only the dog was newish, clearly having been inspired by a "poodle petticoat" that had appeared in *LIFE* in December 1951. The white petticoat with black appliqué poodles was nearly identical to the skirt in the pattern, except for the fact that it was underwear, not outerwear.

Poodles were already synonymous with all things French; the dog appliqué gave the Dior-inspired skirt a meta appeal. The pictorial poodle skirt grew so popular so fast that its novelty—and its name—quickly faded as skirts bearing appliquéd dachshunds, Scottie dogs, and non-canine animals and other imagery soon appeared. In October 1953, *LIFE* reported that "the wide felt skirt, gaily decorated with anything from families of fur poodles to rhinestone phone numbers, is referred to in the garment trade as 'a conversation circle' because it gets its wearer talked to or about at cocktail parties." New York designer Bettie Murrie designed one decorated with a functioning backgammon board, with a pocket shaped like an oversized die to hold the playing pieces. "Purchasers of her new designs will sit on the floor, spread their skirts out around them and passersby will sit down beside them for a hemside round of their favorite game."

Like most fads, these "conversation circles" were short-lived. By 1954, the poodle skirt was in the doghouse; it transitioned out of women's wardrobes and could only be found in the children's department. Just three years later, Dior himself was dead. In his short career, he built a legacy that looms disproportionately large over fashion history. The poodle skirt may have been a passing fancy, but its inspiration, the New Look, was a turning point—a fashion revolution so complete that the shock of it will never grow old.

7

THE NAKED DRESS

Daring to Bare

It wasn't her birthday suit, but it was close. On May 19, 1962, Marilyn Monroe took the stage at a Democratic Party fundraiser at Madison Square Garden to sing "Happy Birthday" to President John F. Kennedy, who would soon turn forty-five. She dropped her fur stole, revealing a glittering, floor-length gown made of sheer, flesh-toned marquisette studded with 2,500 rhinestones.

From the audience, it looked like she was wearing nothing *but* rhinestones. Even without undergarments, the dress was so tight that Monroe reportedly had to be sewn into it. Kennedy joked afterward: "I can now retire from politics after having had 'Happy Birthday' sung to me in such a sweet, wholesome way." It wasn't just Marilyn's breathy, suggestive delivery; it was the dress.

Jean Louis, the French-born Hollywood costume designer behind the gown, called it an "illusion dress"; it created the "illusion" of nudity. He'd achieved a similar sartorial sleight of hand with the strapless dress he conjured up for Rita Hayworth in *Gilda* (see Chapter 5). Monroe contacted him after he made Marlene Dietrich a series of illusion dresses—covered in strategically placed sequins, beads, and lace—to wear in her

FIGURE 17. Marilyn Monroe wore a Jean Louis "illusion dress" to sing "Happy Birthday" to President John F. Kennedy at Madison Square Garden in 1962. (*PictureLux / The Hollywood Archive / Alamy Stock Photo*)

cabaret concerts. It was a look synonymous with Hollywood glamour: costume designers like Walter Plunkett, Edith Head, and Irene all made sheer gowns for the screen. Orry-Kelly had dressed Monroe in one in 1959's *Some Like It Hot*; she crooned "I'm Through with Love" atop a grand piano in a clinging nude silk jersey and black souffle cocktail dress embellished with black sequins, beads, and fringe. The sequins on the sheer décolletage just barely covered her nipples, but the plunging back, which exposed the tops of her buttocks, was even more daring.

At the time, the Hollywood studio system tended to reduce actresses to their most salient body parts. Jane Russell was "The Bust." Vikki Dougan was "The Back." Anita Colby was "The Face." Jean Harlow and Veronica Lake were "The Blonde Bombshell" and "The Peekaboo Girl," for their signature hairstyles. Bette Davis was known for her eyes, and Dietrich was famous for her legs, whether clad in a man's evening suit or a sheer Jean Louis gown. The Paramount publicity department perpetuated the (false) rumor that they were insured by Lloyd's of London. In a 1958 press release, though, Dietrich's publicist highlighted the luxury rather than the legginess of the "diamond-studded dress of moving beads, rhinestones, crystal beads, and diamond droplets" Jean Louis made for the star's stint at the Sahara in Las Vegas.[1] The purported $25,000 price tag—and the "diamonds"—were obvious lies. (It was more like $8,000.) But the emphasis on its opulence is telling. Dietrich came from a noble German family and often played aristocrats on-screen. She may have experimented with gender roles, on- and off-screen, but even in pants she always looked expensive and aloof. On a curvaceous figure like Monroe's—"Jell-O on springs," as it's described in *Some Like It Hot*—the illusion created by a sheer, sequined dress was very different.

Today, they're known as "naked dresses," not "illusion dresses." The term—originally applied to strapless dresses in the late 1930s (see Chapter 5)—gained fresh traction in 1998 thanks to an early episode of HBO's *Sex and the City,* in which protagonist Carrie Bradshaw wears a skimpy, flesh-colored dress for her first date with Mr. Big (see Plate 12). Her prim friend Charlotte disapprovingly calls it "the naked dress." But Carrie's dress isn't really recognizable as a Jean Louis–style evening gown, or even what we could call a "naked dress" today. Instead, it's a slip dress, short but not transparent, with a plunging back. The only illusion is that the dress seems to stay up by magic, supported by barely-there spaghetti straps. Its hue is the matte putty color of an ACE bandage rather than the glowing rose gold of actress Sarah Jessica Parker's skin; it's a slip dress in cut, but also in the sense that it's the same uncanny-valley "nude" tone of a mass-produced foundation garment. It doesn't mimic nudity so much as underwear.

"Naked dress" may be an oxymoron, but it's an apt description for a genre of dresses that bare (or appear to bare) as much as they conceal, whether because they're sheer, flesh-toned, skintight, or all of the above. They may have slits, cutouts, plunging necklines, or pasties. The jewel-studded off-white gown Kendall Jenner wore to the 2015 MuchMusic Video Awards was long-sleeved and opaque, but it had two slits up to her waist, baring both legs and then some, an effect heightened by the deep purple lining. The naked dress may or may not mimic nakedness, but it almost always requires nakedness in the sense of going without undergarments; regardless of how sheer, slashed, or skintight it may be, the dress is designed to reveal that the wearer is naked *beneath* the dress. Once worn only by burlesque performers, it migrated to movie studios, where unfortunate lighting could be carefully controlled. The naked dress went mainstream when it got JFK's presidential seal of approval, and it's been a mainstay of the runway and the red carpet ever since.

Of course, now that the red carpet largely functions as an extension of the runway, it may be hard to believe that celebrities didn't always set fashion trends. Under the studio system, in-house costume designers (rather than couturiers) often dressed actresses for movie premieres and awards shows. But the collapse of the studio system in the late 1960s left celebrities to their own devices—"for better or for worse."[2] It was the era of Cher and Elizabeth Taylor in over-the-top glitz; Demi Moore and Geena Davis in awkward self-designed ensembles; and Barbra Streisand in Arnold Scaasi's transparent bellbottoms. Not until Giorgio Armani arrived in Beverly Hills in 1988 did good taste—and free (borrowed) gowns—begin to return to the red carpet. Other fashion designers followed his example, collaborating with stars, stylists, and jewelers to perform the role once handled by studio costume departments. Today, designer samples appear at movie premieres and awards shows long before they go on sale, and images of the most famous and beautiful women in the world wearing them are instantly broadcast around the world.

With so many designers clamoring for publicity—and so many photographers and journalists eager to give it to them— celebrities must go to ever-greater lengths to get noticed and photographed. The physical fitness boom that began in the

1970s (and a corresponding spike in elective plastic surgery) helped women to achieve perfect bodies without corsets, girdles, or other foundation garments (see Chapter 10). Considering the confluence of these factors—designer freebies and the fitness industrial complex—the naked dress doesn't seem like an oxymoron but an inevitability. It's a style that only needs one accessory: a body worth seeing. Walking the fine line between exposure and overexposure, it flips the script on Hollywood's historic double standards, which have sexualized female bodies while allowing men to keep covered up. In a naked dress, a woman can be both clothed and unclothed, revealing exactly as much skin as she wants.

From its sequined showgirl roots, the naked gown transitioned seamlessly into the anything-goes 1960s. Actress Carroll Baker—leaning into her sexpot image—turned to her friend Dietrich for advice when promoting her 1964 film *The Carpetbaggers*. "I asked if she would mind if I copied one of her costume ideas," Baker wrote in her 1983 autobiography, *Baby Doll*. "A slinky, net-and-chiffon transparent gown with jewels." Dietrich gave her blessing and recommended her to couturier Pierre Balmain. She advised her to "remember the importance of standing on your feet in the sheath and supervising the placement of every single jewel. Your body will be shown to the best advantage if you carefully select what you show and don't show. So don't be a lazy girl."

Baker wore the gown to the film's Hollywood premiere and "caused a sensation," she remembered. "I looked gorgeous—sparkling and devastatingly daring. I wore nothing underneath, and the skin-colored net and chiffon blended under the bright lights with my own flesh just as Marlene had predicted it would. I believe every newspaper in the world printed a photograph of me in that transparent dress." Baker wore similarly sheer gowns to the film's Denver and London premieres. She told syndicated gossip columnist Hedda Hopper that "many designers have leotards to wear underneath, but that's cheating. I skip breakfast and lunch because I don't dare put on an extra ounce." The naked look was both democratic and unforgiving; it "doesn't emphasize any particular part of your anatomy—it gives the entire silhouette," Baker added. Ironically, however, it was an opaque Balmain trouser-and-tank-top ensemble that Baker wore to the 1965 Golden Globes that was "instantly labeled outrageous" and drew "whispers of shocked disapproval," Baker remembered. The Associated Press called the "sequin-covered pajamas" the "sartorial shocker of the evening." Clearly, it was better to go naked than to wear pants.

Balmain predicted that "the new look will be transparent," Hopper reported. He wasn't the only designer to bet on bare. Thanks to the new synthetic materials developed after World War II, fabric could reveal as much as it concealed. Sometimes, these daring designs were worn with elasticized flesh-colored undergarments, but not always. Even as Baker was posing in her glitzy embroidered Balmain gowns, couturier André Courrèges was launching couture into the Space Age with futuristic fashions and fibers, including transparent plastic and netting (see Chapter 8). Yves Saint Laurent's 1967 collection included a sheer black chiffon gown with a fringe of ostrich feathers clustered around the hips, like a grass skirt. A few years later, he interpreted his signature shirtdress in sheer black, worn over leopard-print shorts; patch pockets over the breasts gave it a modicum of modesty. Oscar de la Renta included sheer organza and chiffon blouses in his Spring/Summer 1969 collection, "for any woman who can wear them."[3] Zandra Rhodes tapped into hippie chic with flowing, sheer chiffon maxi dresses; the handcrafting craze brought peekaboo macramé and crocheted gowns. Even Norman Hartnell, best known for dressing Queen Elizabeth, got on the bare bandwagon, including a black crêpe gown dubbed "Sideshow" in his Spring 1971 collection. "A long, wide slither of flesh surfaced from ankle to waist as the designer cut out a side panel and strung the gap with lacing," the Associated Press reported. Though shocking for its time, the dress would not be out of place on the red carpet today.

The chic nudity of the late 1960s began to look tawdry by the 1970s; hemlines dropped, and women began to cover up, choosing evening gowns that were body-conscious but not bare. The naked dress retreated back into show business. Bob Mackie considered himself a costume designer rather than a fashion designer; his references were Old Hollywood screen sirens like Marilyn Monroe, Joan Crawford, and Dietrich, who became his client. Dietrich also inspired another actress-singer Mackie dressed, on-screen and off: Cher. "I was crazy about Marlene from the first time I saw her on the screen," Cher testified. She even shaved off her eyebrows so she could pencil them in to look like Dietrich's, a look that lasted for a whole season of *The Sonny and Cher Show*. Cher often sported showgirl-inspired styles with elaborate headpieces, plunging necklines, cutouts, and crop tops to show off her enviable abs. But when she wore Mackie's sheer, sparkling naked dresses, she was channeling one specific showgirl, Dietrich.

Cher ended up modeling one of those naked dresses—an

iridescent beaded gown trimmed in white feathers that she'd worn to the 1974 Met Gala, escorted by Mackie—on the cover of *Time* later that year, under the headline "Glad Rags to Riches." The reporter suggested that "to a degree, designer Robert Mackie's clothes still make the star." To which Cher retorted: "I wear my clothes; my clothes don't wear me." Mackie told *Vogue*: "It created a lot of hubbub. In those days, *Time* reserved its covers for world leaders or someone who invented something important, like a vaccine. Then there was Cher on the cover in that incredible piece of clothing, and newsstands sold out of it almost immediately. Some cities even banned it from being sold." The Richard Avedon cover image was deemed "pornographic" in Tampa. But Mackie told *TV-Radio Mirror*: "It's really quite a decent dress"—meaning the opposite of "indecent." He explained: "Everything blends into everything else and you're never quite sure what you're seeing. It has a high neckline, no cleavage at all except for the areas that you can see through, and the beads are placed so that you don't see anything. The back *is* low—down to the waist; but so is Cher's hair." As Carroll Baker had discovered, the naked dress doesn't "emphasize any particular part" of the female anatomy; it forces the eye to rove, taking in the whole silhouette and a general impression of nudity that is more illusion than reality. Nevertheless, Cher's Met Gala gown was one of her most daring collaborations with Mackie—and one of the most beautiful, especially in motion.

Like many extreme fashion eras, the over-the-top 1980s led to a backlash in the 1990s. ("Sink to your knees and start atoning for the acquisitive 1980s," *Vogue* commanded its readers in August 1993.) Grunge and minimalism may have been

the buzzwords of the day, but these austere, often androgynous trends were not entirely devoid of dresses; women played
with gender signals, pairing slim, satiny slips and girlish floral
dresses with aggressive leather jackets, platform sneakers, and
combat boots. Amid the stripped-down, body-conscious minimalism of the decade, the naked dress made a comeback. The
shimmering, see-through silver slip dress Kate Moss wore to
an Elite Model Look of the Year party in London in 1993 (accessorized with a pair of black briefs and a cigarette) didn't reveal
anything the world hadn't seen before; the shock of her topless 1992 Calvin Klein ad campaign with Mark Wahlberg had
hardly worn off. But in a room full of statuesque models, her
daringly deconstructed dress was a powerful reminder of the
waifish figure that had made Moss famous, and that fashion curator Colleen Hill has identified as part of "a turn toward reality
and away from the polished, unattainable perfection of 1980s
supermodels," which helped to expand the definition of female
beauty.[4] The dress projected a supremely cool confidence, even
if it can be partly attributed to ignorance; when getting ready
for the party, Moss hadn't realized the borrowed Liza Bruce
dress was transparent. "I had no idea why everyone was so
excited," she confessed to *Vogue*.

Nineties nakedness took on many forms beyond transparency. The *Oxford English Dictionary* credits the first published
use of the term "side boob" (alt. "sideboob") to *Saturday Night
Live* cast member Mike Myers, who used it in a January 30,
1994, interview with *The Sunday Times*. He was referring to his
first glimpse of the elusive anatomical region, on a poster of
actress Farrah Fawcett (likely the one for her 1979 film *Sunburn*, in which her sleeveless wetsuit is unzipped to just below

her breasts). But 1994 was also the year Elizabeth Hurley wore her Versace safety pin gown (see Chapter 3) and the sideboob emerged as a new erogenous zone, piggybacking on the rise of the naked dress. By the early 2000s, sideboob was the new cleavage, the subject of think pieces in *Salon* and *The New York Times*. "Part of its appeal is that it hints at revealing something, and offers the tantalizing possibility of a wardrobe malfunction, while also keeping its wearer covered up," *Salon* explained in November 2015. "It's provocative without putting it all out there." For women with modest cleavage, it was a chic way to show some skin. And, as naked dresses crowded the red carpet, a glimpse of sideboob offered more mystery and novelty than transparency or a plunging neckline.

Actress Gwyneth Paltrow—perhaps trying to dispel memories of the princessy pink Ralph Lauren gown she'd worn to the 1999 Academy Awards ceremony—chose an edgy, punk-inspired Alexander McQueen gown for the 2002 Oscars. The black mesh bodice bared her nipples; her heavy black eyeliner and messy milkmaid braid looked more gimmicky than Goth. McQueen thought she looked "incredible." But critics called it a fashion disaster for the usually stylish star. Paltrow later admitted on her website, Goop: "I should have worn a bra." The next time she went bare on the red carpet—at the *Iron Man 3* premiere—she played it safer; her Space-Age Antonio Berardi gown design had sheer black sleeves and sheer black panels on both sides, but the front and back were opaque. Sideboob? Yes. Nipples? No. Nevertheless, the panels made it impossible to wear underwear of any kind; the *Daily Mail* called it the "most vulgar, look-at-me, attention-seeking dress" ever seen on the red carpet. But there would be many more naked dresses to come.

Not every naked dress is meant to be one. The term "wardrobe malfunction" became a euphemism for accidental nudity after the 2004 Super Bowl halftime show, when Janet Jackson's bare breast was revealed to a live television audience of 140 million people. But wardrobe malfunctions (or "nip slips," a term used as early as 2002, according to *Merriam-Webster*) are nothing new. At the 1969 premiere of her movie *Slogan*, British actress Jane Birkin was photographed in a long-sleeved, short-skirted sweaterdress that turned transparent under the paparazzi's flashbulbs. Birkin told French *Vogue* she didn't realize the dress was transparent—and, if she had known, she would not have worn "knickers." When Lady Diana Spencer was photographed teaching preschool in 1980, backlit in a thin skirt worn without a slip, it was a rare fashion faux pas. The first rule of the naked dress is to know you're wearing a naked dress. Yet accidents involving bright lights and deceptively opaque fabrics continue to happen. In 2018, model-actress Emily Ratajkowski—who has happily worn naked dresses on the red carpet—posted a picture of herself dressed for an Emmy Awards after-party on Instagram with the caption: "Real friends take flash pics to see how sheer your dress is before you leave the house."

The naked dress trend was directly responsible for one of the major innovations to come out of Silicon Valley: Google Images. When Jennifer Lopez attended the 2000 Grammy Awards ceremony in Los Angeles in a plunging, sheer silk Versace gown held up by nothing more than a citrine brooch and double-sided tape, she literally broke the internet (see Plate 13). "At the time, it was the most popular search query we had ever seen," former Google CEO Eric Schmidt remembered.[5] "But we had no surefire way of getting users exactly what they wanted: J.Lo wearing that dress." Search results were limited to simple pages of text with links; Google realized that the website needed an image search tool and developed one, introduced on July 12, 2001. The dress that launched Google Images raised the bar for red-carpet style and, more than a decade before Instagram, prefigured the role of social media in setting fashion trends (and spreading NSFW photos). While Google Images probably would have happened eventually without Lopez, her dress demanded attention because "it was revealing without revealing anything," according to fashion journalist Robin Givhan. "It dazzled because it threatened to slip away at any moment."[6] It was the promise rather than the presence of nakedness that fired imaginations and keyboards.

The role of the red carpet in accelerating the rise of the naked dress cannot be overstated. While only a few photographers might be allowed inside a party or awards show, a huge number could pack the media pen of a red carpet, using stepladders and risers to get a favorable vantage point; increasingly, their footage got livestreamed or published online within seconds. The "step-and-repeat"—the term for a temporary wall or banner plastered with sponsor logos, which came into use in the early 2000s—turned the red carpet into a live commercial, for the actress and her designer as much as the event itself. With its audacity and now-you-see-it visual appeal, the naked dress demanded attention.

By 2015, the Met Gala red carpet would boast three naked

dresses, worn by Lopez (in Versace, her breasts and genitals covered by the coils of an embroidered red dragon), Beyoncé (in sheer, bejeweled Givenchy), and Kim Kardashian (in a white, feathered homage to Cher's Met Gala gown, by Peter Dundas for Roberto Cavalli). Kardashian (who has said she considers Cher a fashion role model) took the naked dress a step further in 2019, attending the Met Gala in a latex Thierry Mugler dress that was not just short, skintight, and nude in hue, but appeared to be dripping wet, an illusion created by beaded crystals that hung from the dress like drops of water. Her hair was styled in glistening gelled waves to match the outfit, and her skin was dewy with oil—an aesthetic inspired by the California surf and Sophia Loren's 1957 film *Boy on a Dolphin*. While the trompe l'oeil look was in keeping with the Gala's theme, "Camp: Notes on Fashion," social media labeled it the "glazed croissant dress."

Defenders of the naked dress often describe it as an instrument of female sexual agency rather than a stereotypically sexy "thirst trap"—a slang term dating to 2011, which implies both desperate lust and desperate attention-seeking. But it can also make powerful statements that have nothing to do with fashion or female sexuality. When actress Halle Berry wore Elie Saab's burgundy gown with a sweeping satin skirt and a sheer bodice decorated with strategically placed bands of floral embroidery to the 2002 Academy Awards ceremony, the revealing gown raised eyebrows on the red carpet. Though Berry had one of the most famous bodies in Hollywood, the bombshell look was at odds with the dramatic role for which she was nominated, in the feel-bad film *Monster's Ball*. But later that night, when Berry became the first (and, to date, only) Black woman to win the Best Actress Oscar, it suddenly seemed fitting that she'd proudly displayed her skin on a red carpet that has not always been welcoming to Black women. Berry may have been referencing that history-making night when she attended the 2018 NAACP Image Awards in another burgundy naked dress, by Reem Acra—but this time the sheer fabric was on her bottom half, with just a strip of lace for modesty.

As a fashion and makeup entrepreneur, Barbados-born actress-singer Rihanna has been outspoken about offering options for a wide range of sizes and skin tones. She has also demonstrated that she's comfortable in her own dark skin on the red carpet. When she accepted the 2014 Fashion Icon Award from the Council of Fashion Designers of America, she lived up to her new title by going naked. Her sheer Adam Selman dress was studded with 230,000 Swarovski crystals and had an embellished headscarf and gloves to match. She wore nothing else but a flesh-toned thong, which she later said she wished she'd had bedazzled to match the dress. In her acceptance speech, Rihanna revealed: "Even as a child I remember thinking, 'She can beat me, but she cannot beat my outfit.' And to this day that's how I think about it: I can compensate for all of my weaknesses with my fashion!" Her dress underlined her naked confidence. "I will not back down from being a woman, from being black, from having an opinion," the star told *T* magazine in 2019.

Canadian model Winnie Harlow, who shot to fame in 2014 as a contestant on *America's Next Top Model,* has the skin condition vitiligo, which causes uneven, patchy pigmentation. After being bullied as a child, Harlow became a public spokesperson for vitiligo as well as appearing in fashion magazines, commercials, and music videos. When Harlow wears a naked dress—as she has on several occasions, both for red-carpet events and photo shoots—she is baring more than her figure; she's baring her unique skin, knowing it will make some people uncomfortable regardless of what she's wearing. Harlow uses fashion—what it conceals and reveals—to challenge expectations about beauty, race, and the female body and present herself as a work of art.

Just when it seemed like the naked dress had bared all its secrets, Jennifer Lopez closed the Versace Spring/Summer 2020 fashion show in Milan wearing an updated version of the green gown she'd made iconic twenty years earlier. The dress hadn't aged and neither, it seemed, had Lopez, who had recently turned fifty. There was no hiding the naked truth that a woman of five decades could still be a thirst trap and flaunt it in a dress that proudly celebrated her body. The collection commemorated the twentieth anniversary of Versace's "Jungle" print. The parade of dresses lush with leafy green vines and palm fronds evoked the Garden of Eden, where Eve, having eaten from the tree of knowledge, covered her nudity with fig leaves. But these women were naked and unashamed.

8

THE MINISKIRT

Fashion's Final Frontier

The frenzy that greeted the arrival of the miniskirt in 1964 made controversies over strapless necklines seem quaint. But the miniskirt was never intended to be sexy. Shocking, yes. However, the glamazon in high heels, a push-up bra, and a short, tight skirt—think Sharon Stone in *Basic Instinct*—is a relatively recent cliché (see Chapter 10). The miniskirt of the 1960s was about youth, not sex. It was always worn with flats, and it usually looked like something purchased in the children's department, with a simple A-line silhouette and playful, almost juvenile styling. Its sexual power—and danger—lay not in what it revealed, but in what it represented. It was "the most self-indulgent, optimistic 'look at me, isn't life wonderful' fashion ever devised," according to British designer Mary Quant, one of its foremost proponents. "It expressed the sixties, the emancipation of women, the Pill, and rock 'n' roll. . . . It was the beginning of women's lib."[1]

Women's hemlines had been rising—and falling again—

since the 1920s. While the "hemline index"—the idea that fluctuating skirt lengths predict the direction of the stock market—is a fallacy, hemlines are often reliable indicators of changing lifestyles and moral standards (see Chapter 2). After plunging to calf-length with the New Look, hemlines began creeping up again in the late 1950s. Christian Dior's carefully constructed corsetry gave way to the simplicity of Cristóbal Balenciaga's loose-fitting "sack" dress, which was voluminous on top and tight at the knee, its off-kilter proportions drawing attention to the shorter hemline. In 1959, Yves Saint Laurent's equally waistless "Trapeze" collection for Dior turned the sack on its head, its wide A-line ending abruptly below the knee, highlighting slim calves and prefiguring the shorter skirts of the following decade.

The post–World War II baby boom had created a "youthquake"; by the midsixties, roughly 40 percent of the American and British populations were under twenty-five. France, Canada, Australia, and New Zealand experienced similarly seismic demographic shifts. After years of wartime austerity—that, in some cases, dragged on long after World War II actually ended—their economies were finally booming, too. With military service no longer compulsory, the sizeable younger generation had more time as well as more money than the previous generation. A new wave of rock and roll music captured the energy and optimism of the era.

Fashion expressed it, too. "There was a time when every girl under twenty yearned to look like an experienced, sophisticated thirty," Quant wrote in her 1966 autobiography. "All this is in reverse with a vengeance now. Suddenly every girl with a hope of getting away with it is aiming not only to look under voting age but under the age of consent." This wasn't just a step forward but a pushback against the social and sartorial conservatism of the 1950s. "We'd been stilted in the 1950s," *Sunday Times* fashion writer Meriel McCooey reflected. "Coming out of the war everything felt so stuffy and heavy. You felt that you were encased in your clothes, they were so inhibiting; even the underwear was inhibiting."[2] Young women dressed like their mothers, complete with hats, gloves, and girdles; they had no choice. "Fashion in the late 1950s was definitely for thirty-year-olds and over," complained Barbara Hulanicki, owner of the seminal London boutique Biba. "To get yourself clad in something nice then seemed virtually impossible. . . . There was little specially designed for the young."[3] That was about to change. "The sixties began in deceptive quiet on the fashion front," fashion editor Ernestine Carter remembered. "It was the quiet of a pan of milk about to boil."[4]

The Soviets may have launched the Sputnik satellite in 1957, but—as far as the fashion world was concerned—the Space Age didn't take off until 1964, when André Courrèges launched models in helmet-shaped hats, metallic jumpsuits, and short, flat-soled, white "moon boots" down a Paris catwalk. Trained as a civil engineer before serving as a pilot in World War II, Courrèges spent a decade working for Balenciaga; his Basque heritage gained him entrée to the otherwise all-Spanish house. There, he internalized Balenciaga's dictate that "elegance is elimination." After founding his own label in 1961, Courrèges set about eliminating bras ("which in ten years will be as forgotten as whalebone corsets are today," he predicted in 1965) and hiking hemlines, showing "the way toward the mini with the shortest skirts in Paris," according to Carter.[5] In his "Moon

FIGURE 18. Actress Claudine Auger, wearing an André Courrèges minidress and moon boots, stops traffic in Paris in the summer of 1965. (*Everett Collection*)

Girl" collection, shown in April 1964, Courrèges raised hemlines to the stratosphere, envisioning a futuristic space-scape of man-made materials, unisex garments, and geometric silhouettes. While the most daring skirts of the 1920s tended to cover the knees, these bared them, and then some, dramatically altering the proportions of the fashionable female body. "The boots were intended for aesthetic adjustment," fashion journalist Marylin Bender explained. "Piecemeal Courrèges was a catastrophe. The total look of Courrèges, however, was a synonym for contemporary."[6]

Astronauts wore white because it made them visible against the black expanse of space; Courrèges's "little white dresses," as he called them, represented an optimistic vision of a utopian future, as well as new textile technologies that made it possible to produce optical whites suggestive of scientists' lab coats and the moon's fluorescence. *Vogue* called it "the pure white theater of the new." *LIFE* dubbed the designer "Lord of the Space Ladies." French *Vogue* hailed "the Courrèges revolution," demanding: "Are you for it or against it?" There was no middle ground. Courrèges's out-of-this-world collection was both incendiary and invigorating. "His controversial pants suits, above-the-knee skirts, and sleek mid-calf boots have aroused much excitement since they were introduced last season," *The New York Times* reported in August 1964. "They made sense and, at the same time, gave women a bold new perspective about their lives." Designers like Paco Rabanne, Pierre Cardin, and Rudi Gernreich followed Courrèges's lead. While many of his ideas—like those helmet hats, or his transparent tulle "pantacourt," a shorts romper—were ahead of their time, his above-the-knee skirt had legs.

Despite his aviation background, Courrèges's "space aesthetic" celebrated "space travel imagery without consideration of its practical realities," and thus owed more to science fiction than science, Barbara Brownie has observed.[7] The first female astronaut, Soviet cosmonaut Valentina Tereshkova, had already flown to space in 1963, wearing a unisex blue zip-front jumpsuit, not a white miniskirt. But short skirts had been a feature of science fiction since the 1940s, part of a creative futurism that envisioned women as essential, empowered crew members on space missions. *Space Patrol*, the groundbreaking television series that debuted in 1950, was as notable for its strong female characters as for their short hemlines and flat-soled boots. And Courrèges certainly inspired Hardy Amies's costumes for *2001: A Space Odyssey*, released in 1968. (In the same year, Paco Rabanne dressed Jane Fonda as Barbarella in skimpy bodysuits, a sexier vision of spacewear.)

In 1966, *Star Trek* premiered and the USS *Enterprise* took flight with a miniskirted chief communications officer, Lieutenant Nyota Uhura (see Plate 14). In contrast to Courrèges's pristine white, the show's costumes (designed by William Theiss) used bold primary colors, a subtle ploy to encourage viewers to upgrade their black-and-white sets to RCA's new color televisions. But the minidresses, go-go boots, and knit jumpsuits echoed Courrèges and Cardin. Actress Nichelle Nichols, who played Uhura, said that "in later years, especially as the women's movement took hold in the seventies, people began to ask me about my costume. Some thought it 'demeaning' for a woman in the command crew to be dressed so sexily." Nichols found this surprising. "Contrary to what many may think today, no one really saw it as demeaning back then," she explained. "In fact, the miniskirt was a symbol of sexual liberation. More to the point, though, in the twenty-third century, you are respected for your abilities regardless of what you do or do not wear."[8] Indeed, Courrèges felt that couture had failed women. "You don't walk through life anymore," he told *Women's Wear Daily* in July 1972. "You run. You dance. You drive a car. You take a plane, not a train. Clothes must be able to move, too." Compared to the poodle skirts and pencil skirts of the 1950s, the mini was made to move.

Of course, it didn't take a cosmically minded couturier to put the miniskirt on the map; as early as 1958, young women in London—far from the rarified world of Parisian couture— were already shortening their skirts. Designer Mary Quant was an early ambassador of the "above the knee" look, sporting a knee-skimming skirt during a visit to New York in 1960. In his own eyes, Courrèges was "the man who invented the mini. Mary Quant only commercialized the idea." But Quant insisted that it was inevitable. "It wasn't me or Courrèges who invented the miniskirt. . . . It was the girls in the street who did it."[9] Quant, however, deserves credit for the name. The term "miniskirt" didn't appear in print until 1965, and it was likely coined by Quant, whose favorite car was the Mini Cooper.

Cynics predicted that the shocking style wouldn't outlast its first summer, but, as temperatures dropped, hemlines stayed put. Women determined to brave the cold in miniskirts simply added thick, colorful tights and boots. The miniskirt graduated from nightclubs to college campuses and office buildings, getting shorter and shorter along the way; first it bared the knees, then the lower thigh, then the entire leg. Photos show that hemlines reached their highest point—six or seven inches above the knee—by 1966. (Photographic evidence is essential to studying the rise and fall of hemlines, as many surviving dresses made in the early 1960s had their skirts truncated at a later date.) In 1967, one New York designer quipped to *Time*: "There is the micromini, the micro-micro, the 'Oh, My God,' and the 'Hello, Officer.'"

Quant opened her own boutique, Bazaar, in the bohemian Chelsea neighborhood in 1955. Bazaar was not a couture house, a department store, or a chain; it was something entirely new. It functioned as a gathering place as much as a retail outlet. Dancers, musicians, mods, and beatniks were drawn to Quant's witty window displays, which showed miniskirted mannequins posed in surreal tableaux. Quant originally intended to sell other people's clothing designs, but she became frustrated with the available options and began attending evening sewing classes so she could make her own merchandise. She had an innate flair for design, effortlessly mixing prints and textures while incorporating industrial touches like contrasting topstitching and visible zipper pulls. "By 1960 Mary was inventing, no longer just reflecting what she saw on the King's Road," remembered Ernestine Carter of *Harper's Bazaar*. "She was creating her own Look—a Look that jolted England out of its conventional attitude toward clothes. She was the first to express a mood that swept the world."[10]

By 1967, there were more than two thousand such "boutiques" in London, and British street style was internationally recognized as the Chelsea Look or the London Look. "France was way behind," Balenciaga's biographer Mary Blume pointed out. "The word boutique may be French but the idea of helter-skelter cheap fashion in kooky little shops was not."[11] Courrèges and Yves Saint Laurent—who had opened his Rive Gauche ready-to-wear boutique in 1966—were trying to change that. But British boutique culture was closer to today's fast fashion than traditional ready-to-wear; Bazaar's stock was constantly refreshed, simply because the clothes sold as fast as Quant could make them. The general consensus among the younger generation (and the media that catered to them) was that haute couture was dying, if not already dead.

Quant proposed a radical alternative, introducing youthful, wearable dresses and suits in unexpected proportions, colors, and textiles. She broke all the rules of dress decorum, using formal fabrics for casual clothes and winter fabrics for summer styles. Her simple silhouettes didn't require corsets, waspies, or petticoats. Not only did they look different, they challenged the very idea of fashion, making it more individual, playful, and democratic than the haute couture sold across the pond. Though Quant's clothes kept cleavage under wraps, tights became essential accessories as hemlines climbed higher and higher; short skirts exposed the garters used to hold up traditional stockings. But Quant struggled to find the bright hues she needed to match her minis. "Stocking manufacturers did not have the right machinery so I persuaded theatrical manufacturers to make us tights," she wrote in her autobiography. Quant didn't invent tights, but she commercialized them, bringing them out of the dance studio and into the mainstream, in opaque shades of mustard yellow, silver glitter, or wild op-art patterns. When Quant designed a collection for the American department store JCPenney, she "persuaded them that providing a full range of tights/pantyhose, which they previously barely stocked, was vital for the company if they wanted miniskirts to sell in a big way." This strategy was so successful that "they turned all their hosiery buying power toward pantyhose, and were so well positioned to persuade American hosiery manufacturers that tights were the future that they reaped the rewards of this decision alone for years. They made millions."

Like Coco Chanel, Quant designed for herself, and she was her own best advertisement. A young, opinionated working woman with an angular Vidal Sassoon five-point bob, Quant summed up her personal brand of feminism by declaring that "fashion is a tool to compete in life outside the home." She believed that the future was bright—literally. "It was the little dress that was anything but black," said *Daily Mirror* fashion editor Felicity Green. "Color exploded in a way that one had never seen before." Eschewing the head-to-toe black beatnik aesthetic, Quant worked in bold primary colors and op-art prints that suited her short A-line shifts in sculptural fabrics like tweed, bonded wool jersey, and linen-synthetic blends— elements that came to define the London Look. Quant's personal favorite was a zip-front skater dress whose short, flared skirt suggested the grace and athleticism of the ice rink. The point was not to bare women's legs but to liberate them; as Quant put it, women should be able to run to catch a bus. It's no accident that the key purveyors of "youthquake" fashion— Quant, Hulanicki, Marion Foale, and Sally Tuffin, and, in America, Betsey Johnson and Bonnie Cashin—were women. "It was the era of the little dress, and they were little dresses designed for girlies by girlies," Green said. "They were intensely feminine."[12]

World War II had changed women's priorities; even as they enjoyed unprecedented opportunities and freedoms, they yearned for simpler times, even going back to childhood. "To me, adult appearance was very unattractive, alarming and terrifying, stilted, confined, and ugly," Quant said. "It was something I knew I didn't want to grow into."[13] Instead, she dressed women in colorful ruffles, bows, smocks, patch pockets, pinafores, daisy prints, and Peter Pan collars, paired with schoolgirl straw hats, Mary Janes, pigtails, and knee socks. One red dress came with matching ruffled briefs and had a skirt short enough to show them off. High hemlines and waistlines mimicked the cut of children's clothes and made the wearer's legs look miles long. Quant balanced these girlish fantasies with daring menswear touches like silk neckties layered under tiny waistcoats, tailored trousers, and gray flannel skirt suits. A dress in the shape of a long cardigan was inspired by the sweaters Rex Harrison wore onstage as Professor Henry Higgins in *My Fair Lady,* the West End hit musical of 1958. The London Look was both intensely feminine and "incredibly modern and cutting edge," remembered talent agent Sandy Lieberson. "The flat shoes, the tights—everything was about function and not just decorative. It liberated women from the trap of fashion."[14] As former Miss America Bess Myerson told a fashion show audience in 1966: "We used to dress like Jackie Kennedy; now we're dressing like Caroline."[15] Caroline Kennedy was eight years old at the time.

Most of Quant's clients and models were too young to remember World War II, but they had endured its hardships. "They were not used to eating massive meals," Hulanicki remembered in her autobiography. "They were the postwar babies who had been deprived of nourishing protein in childhood and grew up into beautiful skinny people. A designer's dream. It didn't take much for them to look outstanding. The simpler the better, the shorter the better." Wide-eyed, rail-thin ingenues like Penelope Tree and Twiggy modeled the London Look in the pages of British *Vogue*. Twiggy (born Lesley Hornby) shot to fame after the *Daily Express* named her the "Face of '66." She was famous for her cropped hair and slim, "boyish" figure, which, together with her short skirts and flat shoes, gave her the appearance of a modern-day flapper. But she was often dressed in cartoonishly oversized and juvenile clothes. Her enormous eyes with their painted-on eyelashes reinforced an impression of childlike androgyny, like a doll, or a little girl playing dress-up (see Plate 15). Photographers posed her on tricycles, or tugging shyly at her skirts, or throwing herself at the camera, arms outstretched. During interviews, Twiggy frequently reinforced her youthfulness by fidgeting like a nervous schoolgirl and responding to questions with: "I dunno."

The mini got maximum publicity in 1965, when English model Jean Shrimpton, twenty-two, wore one to Derby Day at the Flemington Racecourse in Melbourne, Australia. The Colin Rolfe dress—worn with two-tone slingback flats and, in defiance of race protocol, no hat, gloves, or stockings—caused a scandal at the staid event. (The fact that it was 94 degrees Fahrenheit did not excuse this lapse in fashion etiquette.) Tellingly, Shrimpton's most vocal critic—Lady Nathan, the former mayor of Melbourne's wife—dismissed her in infantilizing terms: "This Shrimpton is a child and she showed very bad manners."[16] Shrimpton retorted in *The Observer*: "I have always worn short skirts and while I am young, I'll go on wearing them." The next day, she arrived at the racecourse in a more conventional outfit but told reporters: "I feel Melbourne isn't

ready for me yet. It seems years behind London." The outcry may have reflected percolating class envy, too; it was well
known that the DuPont textile company had paid Shrimpton
a then-unimaginable £2,000 to travel to Australia to judge
a contest of fashions made with its new Orlon acrylic fiber,
which Rolfe used for the custom dress. Photographers got on
their knees—"like proposing Victorian swains," Shrimpton
said—to make the skirt look even shorter.

Even wedding dresses came up short; miniskirts were especially popular for second weddings, at a time when long gowns
and trains were considered inappropriate for divorcées. Actress
Sharon Tate married director Roman Polanski at the Chelsea Register Office—located on the King's Road, in the heart
of Swinging London—in 1968. The bride wore an ivory silk
moiré minidress trimmed with baby blue velvet ribbon that
she had reportedly designed herself, though it bore the label
of Hollywood custom dressmaker Alba. With its high collar,
Empire waistline, and long, puffed princess sleeves, the dress
reflected the girlish, romantic nostalgia that characterized
late 1960s fashion: baby doll ruffles, bows, pie-frill collars, and
floral prints. "It's Renaissance until you get below the knees,"
Tate told reporters, though it was actually more of a Victorian-
Edwardian hybrid, and the hemline skimmed the tops of her
thighs. Tate "adored miniskirts and looked spectacular in
them," her sister Debra remembered. In lieu of a veil, Tate's
elaborate, upswept blond curls were scattered with pink and
white flowers; she accessorized with sheer white tights and
low-heeled white pumps. Polanski was equally caught up in
the neo-Edwardian trend, sporting an olive-green frock coat
with bell-bottoms and a frilly jabot shirt he'd purchased from

Jack Vernon's Hollywood boutique; one observer described him as "a cross between Little Lord Fauntleroy and Ringo Starr." Maid of honor Barbara Parkins, Tate's costar in *Valley of the Dolls*, wore a crochet minidress almost as short as the bride's.

Raquel Welch wore a similarly daring crochet minidress of incongruously virginal white for her Valentine's Day city hall wedding to her second husband, producer Patrick Curtis, in Paris in 1967—a fashion-forward take on traditional lace. Her knee-length white fur coat was significantly longer than the "peekaboo" dress, which "created pandemonium" among the waiting photographers, *LIFE* reported. Audrey Hepburn wore a pink wool Givenchy minidress (with a matching headscarf rather than a veil) when she married her second husband, Italian psychiatrist Andrea Dotti, at the town hall of Morges, Switzerland, in 1969. In the chic, simple ensemble, paired with white tights and flats, she looked much younger than her thirty-nine years. While their dresses (or rather, their legs) might have looked out of place in a church, as divorcées, all three actresses married at city hall, and all three married in Europe, where all couples were required to have a civil ceremony in addition to the optional religious ceremony. The practice helped normalize the small, informal, but fashion-forward second wedding.

The miniskirt had some notable detractors. Coco Chanel disparaged it, saying: "One already collects too much dust and mud on one's legs in Paris, must one now have it on one's thighs?" Norman Hartnell, dressmaker to Her Majesty Queen Elizabeth II, also disapproved, complaining that most women had knees "like underdone rock cakes"—lumpy English pastries similar to scones.[17] Fashion photographer Cecil Beaton quipped: "Never in the history of fashion has so little material been raised so high to reveal so much that needs to be covered so badly." And Madame Grès found miniskirts "in bad taste."[18] Though women were undeterred and continued to wear the mini, it could not remain at the forefront of fashion for long. By 1970, even Mary Quant had embraced the maxi skirt, which appealed to her love of Victorian and Edwardian styles. Her fans grew out their Sassoon bobs and started wearing a new, more down-to-earth "London Look": flowing skirts in romantic floral textiles by designers like Laura Ashley, Bill Gibb, Ossie Clark, and Jean Muir.

When *Star Trek: The Next Generation* premiered in 1987, the familiar opening-credits mission statement—"To boldly go where no man has gone before"—became gender neutral: "To boldly go where no one has gone before." Creator Gene Roddenberry brought William Theiss back to update the USS Enterprise crew's uniforms for a new generation of viewers. As star Nichelle Nichols had discovered, her original short-skirted uniform hadn't aged well; it no longer seemed empowering, but infantilizing. However, instead of getting rid of the short-skirted dresses—or "skants," in Starfleet parlance—for the show's female leads, Theiss put them on male extras, too, belatedly framing it as a unisex style. Truly, this was fashion's final frontier. But audiences weren't fooled; three seasons in, the "skant" disappeared without explanation, never to return.

PLATE 1. Navy WAVES wearing their Mainbocher-designed summer uniforms visit the USS *Missouri* in August 1944. (*Naval History and Heritage Command*)

PLATE 2. Paul Poiret's neoclassical "Joséphine" dress, illustrated by Paul Iribe in 1908, was named for Empress Joséphine. (*Wikimedia Commons*)

PLATE 3. Geraldine Chaplin wore one of her mother's Delphos gowns and shawls in the Spanish film *Mamá cumple 100 años* (1979). (*Photo 12 / Alamy Stock Photo*)

TOP LEFT: PLATE 4. Madame Grès aspired to be a sculptor, and called her Grecian-inspired gowns—like this one from 1962—"living sculptures." (*Arthur Tracy Cabot Fund, Museum of Fine Arts, Boston [www.mfa.org]*)

TOP RIGHT: PLATE 5. Issey Miyake collaborated with artist Yasumasa Morimura on *Pleats Please Guest Artist Series, no. 1,* a 1997 dress juxtaposing a neoclassical Ingres painting with a photo of the artist on Miyake's pleated polyester. (*Gift of the artist, Rhode Island Scho of Design Museum [CC0 1.0]*)

LEFT: PLATE 6. First Lady Michelle Obama's 2009 inaugural ball gown by Jason Wu suggested new beginnings as well as evoking the ancient roots of democracy. (*REUTERS / Alamy Stock Photo*)

TOP LEFT: PLATE 7. After her *Black Panther*-inspired catsuit caused a controversy, Serena Williams wore a tutu designed by Virgil Abloh for Nike in her semifinal victory at the 2018 U.S. Open. (*UPI / Alamy Stock Photo*)

TOP RIGHT: PLATE 8. There was nothing funereal about the little black Versace dress Elizabeth Hurley wore to the premiere of *Four Weddings and a Funeral* (1994). (*Tim Rooke / Shutterstock.com*)

RIGHT: PLATE 9. Princess Diana's little black dress by Christina Stambolian became an instrument of royal revenge in 1994. (*PA Images / Alamy Stock Photo*)

TOP LEFT: PLATE 10. With its wraparound skirt, the Charles James "Taxi" dress of 1931 was as easy to get into and out of as a cab. (*Image copyright © The Metropolitan Museum of Art. Image source: Art Resource, NY*)

TOP RIGHT: PLATE 11. Junya Watanabe reinvented the Bar Suit as a motorcycle jacket and fluted polyurethane skirt in her Autumn/Winter 2011-12 ready-to-wear collection. (*Camera Press Ltd. / Alamy Stock Photo*)

LEFT: PLATE 12. Sarah Jessica Parker wore her *Sex and the City* character's "naked dress" from the set to the 1997 VH1 Vogue Fashion Awards red carpet. (*Getty Images*)

PLATE 13. Jennifer Lopez broke the internet [i]he plunging silk chiffon Versace she wore [t]he 2000 Grammy Awards. (*Featureflash* [Arch]ive / Alamy Stock Photo)

PLATE 14. Actress Nichelle Nichols called Lt. Nyota Uhura's short-skirted *Star Trek* uniform "a symbol of sexual liberation." (*NBC / Photofest*)

PLATE 15. Photographers often infantilized miniskirted model Twiggy with childlike props and accessories like bicycles, jump ropes, pigtails, and Mary Janes. (*Getty Images*)

PLATE 16. The hemline wars played out on the cover of *LIFE* in August 1970. (*John Dominis / The LIFE Picture Collection / Shutterstock.com*)

PLATE 17. Azzedine Alaïa fits a "mummy" dress on Grace Jones in 1985; she would wear his clothes as the villain in the James Bond film *A View to a Kill*, released that year. (*Shutterstock.com*)

PLATE 18. Supermodel Cindy Crawford wore a Hervé Léger "bandage" dress to *Vogue's* 100th anniversary party in 1998. (*Getty Images*)

PLATE 19. Stacey Plaskett, delegate to the House of Representatives from the U.S. Virgin Islands, arrives at the U.S. Capitol to serve as impeachment manager on the second day of former President Donald Trump's 2021 impeachment trial. (*Kevin Dietsch / UPI / Shutterstock.com*)

PLATE 20. Tae kwon do athlete Pita Taufatofua became a social media sensation when he carried Tonga's flag in the 2016 Summer Olympics opening ceremony in Rio de Janeiro, Brazil, wearing little more than coconut oil and a tapa cloth ta'ovala, a traditional Polynesian wrapped skirt. (*REUTERS / Alamy Stock Photo*)

PLATE 21. Nirvana front man Kurt Cobain paired a floral dress with a beard and black eyeliner on the cover of the September 1993 issue of *The Face.* (*TheCoverVersion / Alamy Stock Photo*)

PLATE 22. Activist actor Billy Porter wore a velvet Christian Siriano "tuxedo gown" to the 2019 Oscars. (*Everett Collection Inc. / Alamy Stock Photo*)

9

THE MIDI SKIRT

Divider of Nations

The midi skirt heralded a political and aesthetic revolution in womenswear and a turning point in American consumer culture. In length and in name, the midi was a direct riposte to the mini—a homegrown alternative to an invasive foreign import. By the late 1960s, the once-shocking mini had lost its novelty and was beginning to wear out its welcome; it had grown shorter and shorter until, finally, it had no place to go but down. On June 10, 1968, *Women's Wear Daily* banned miniskirts from the office, explaining in a memo: "We all know minis are dead." *Vogue* editor in chief Diana Vreeland immediately countered: "*Vogue* has made it quite clear that we believe in any length skirt that is becoming to the wearer. The miniskirt looks delicious in the summer with the right legs and the right girl."[1] This heavily qualified endorsement failed to convince readers. It was the beginning of a slow but inexorable backlash against the mini, which *Women's Wear* dubbed the "hemline war."

As the decade spiraled into social and political chaos, women's hemlines—which had once risen and fallen virtually in lockstep with the dictates of fashion magazines—careened from thigh-high to floor-length, hitting every demarcation in between. Minis and maxis jostled for prominence. Designers (and customers) reluctant to commit to one length experimented with asymmetrical hemlines, handkerchief hemlines, and long coats paired with short skirts. Some found fashion's infinite variety freeing; others were frustrated by its ups and downs. But the spirit of anarchy—mirroring the restless mood of the times—was impossible to ignore. Not just hemlines but standards of beauty, prestige, and propriety were in flux. While Seventh Avenue had once collectively dictated seasonal trends to a grateful nation, designers could no longer agree on so much as a standard length. As American society changed—and kept changing—so did the role and meaning of fashion in it.

Amid this hemline hemming and hawing, the midi emerged as a chic and cerebral compromise. Today, the term "midi" is applied to skirts that end just below the knee or mid-calf, and pencil skirts as well as full skirts. But it originally denoted a specific, unforgiving shape: not mid-leg, but mid-calf, widening in an A-line from the waist to four inches below the knee. It was (and is) a tricky silhouette to pull off without looking stumpy or frumpy. With the wrong shoes, it was a disaster. While not as obviously youthful as the mini, it looked best on young, tall, slim women with the confidence to cover up. Like so many fashion trends, it won style points for degree of difficulty as well as for execution.

If the mini epitomized the London Look, many in the American media blamed the midi on the French, who had championed the "longuette" length in the Fall 1969 Paris collections; the midi first began to attract widespread notice in America in 1970, though it was spotted as early as 1968. A more likely source of inspiration could be found closer to home, in Theadora Van Runkle's costumes for the 1967 film *Bonnie and Clyde*, set in Depression-era Texas. Faye Dunaway's instantly iconic berets, clinging sweaters, and calf-length skirts in earthy shades and textures proved an irresistible alternative to microminis in synthetic fabrics and Day-Glo colors. In July 1970, *Show* magazine reflected: "Probably no one imagined at the time that the most far-reaching contribution *Bonnie and Clyde* would leave to our acid-rock-pop generation was its influence on fashion. Nor that Theadora Van Runkle . . . would become responsible for the midis and braless bosoms that are the trademark of the early seventies. But that's just what happened."

Far from saccharine nostalgia, then, the midi represented gritty glamour for fashion outlaws. According to designer Chester Weinberg, who made the midi his signature, it was "a direct reflection of the women's movement. It's for those who don't particularly care about what men think about the way they dress." By 1970, the midi had replaced the mini in fashion magazines and boutiques, if not necessarily in the hearts of consumers. The *New Yorker*'s fashion critic, Kennedy Fraser, crowed: "Hail, Covered Knee! The fashionable woman has long legs and aristocratic ankles but no knees. . . . She wears her skirt around the calf. She welcomes the return of the dress and is happy to find clothes that look new and that are not, perforce, some kind of trouser suit, pajama suit, or jumpsuit. . . . She is tired of looking like an upside-down ice-cream cone with arms and legs."[2] The comparison is telling: while the playful

FIGURE 19. This publicity still from *Bonnie and Clyde* (1967) re-creates a famous 1933 photo of the real Bonnie Parker and Clyde Barrow, with one difference: in the original, Bonnie's skirt reaches her ankles. (*PictureLux / The Hollywood Archive / Alamy Stock Photo*)

mini made women look like children, the midi was ageless, timeless, and romantic.

But if some praised the midi's intellectual or feminist qualities, *Time* magazine condemned it as "ungainly, unflattering, and unwarranted." Coco Chanel called it "awkward" (though she reserved her strongest vitriol for the mini). For many men newly accustomed to seeing the female leg on full display for the first time in history, it was an unwelcome step backward. And women, as fashion writer Bernadine Morris explained, faced "the agonizing decision of choosing short skirts and appearing old-fashioned or wearing long skirts and looking, many of them felt, old."[3]

Even more offensive than the midi's appearance was the marketing push behind it, which seemed oblivious to public opinion. On October 2, 1970, *The Wall Street Journal* summarized the "much-scorned but also much-promoted" style in a damning headline: "Women Call It Sleazy, Dowdy, Depressing; but Designers Say It Will Catch On Yet." Indeed, *The New Yorker* warned that "no amount of protest will stem the tide of the longer skirt"—the fashion industry had already invested too heavily in it. Shoppers looking for miniskirts found racks stuffed with midis, with a few maxis, pantsuits, and gaucho pants (whose full, calf-length silhouette mimicked the midi) thrown in for variety. Bonwit Teller even banned its saleswomen from wearing minis on the shop floor.

Ironically, feminism became the man-repelling midi's worst enemy; women were no longer prepared to purchase whole new wardrobes just because the fashion industry told them to. In an October 1970 article titled "Fashion Fascism: The Politics of Midi," the San Francisco counterculture fashion magazine *Rags*

decried the midi as a capitalist "conspiracy"; in addition to being "cumbersome and matronly" it had "built-in obsolescence."[4]
(How this differentiated it from any other fashion trend, the
magazine did not specify.) With inflation on the rise, the midi
was an economic encumbrance, too; the longer length required
a higher price point.

The warring interests of consumers, retailers, and the
fashion press culminated in what *Newsweek* called "the midi-
skirt debacle of 1970." In March, a group calling itself GAMS
("Girls Against More Skirt") picketed on Seventh Avenue, carrying placards reading LEGS! LEGS! LEGS!; across the country, in
Beverly Hills, a similar organization—POOFF, or "Preservation of Our Femininity and Finances"—circulated a petition
to "stop this hoax." In April, FADD ("Fight Against Dictating
Designers") staged a "snip-in" in Washington, D.C.; a woman
stood on a table at the busy corner of Connecticut Avenue and
K Street to have a foot of her midi skirt cut off. The stunt was
followed by a march through the city's shopping district; "remnants of the transmogrified skirt fluttered flag-like from a stick
carried by a male marcher," the Associated Press reported. In
a widely covered July incident, miniskirted women picketed
a Miami shopping center carrying signs reading DOWN WITH
THE MIDI and THINGS GO BETTER WITH MINIS. "Toting signs
over their head helps raise the length of their already short
skirts," the Associated Press noted.

The protest—which attracted "middle-aged mommas" as
well as teenagers—was framed as a free speech issue: "They
want freedom of choice in their attire." Many of the "mommas" remembered wearing long skirts in the late 1940s and
1950s and found the midi retrograde rather than modern. Days

FIGURE 20. Miniskirted women march in protest of the new midi length in Miami in 1970, one of many similar protests around the world. (*Jim Kerlin / AP / Shutterstock.com*)

later, a dozen women in miniskirts marched on the New Jersey State House in Trenton. In August, GAMS marched in front of Boston's "most fashionable clothing stores"; UPI reported that "they said mid-calf and longer skirts were an attempt by manufacturers to exploit some women's susceptibility to fashion trends." Days later, *LIFE* magazine put a female shopper on the cover, holding a drab midi skirt up to her Pucci minidress in front of a dressing room mirror under the headline "The Fight to Sell the Midi: Can Dollars and Pressure Prevail?" (See Plate 16.) It predicted: "Farewell to knees and maybe even calves if the anti-mini forces have their way." It quoted retailers behind the plot "to foist the midi on a reluctant public," including Stanley Marcus of Neiman Marcus and Gordon Franklin, president of Saks Fifth Avenue, who all declared the mini dead. Meanwhile, "midi enthusiasts" like Doris Day, *Today Show* host Barbara Walters, and *Women's Wear Daily* publisher James Brady sang the longer length's praises. But the most colorful quotes came from the midi's detractors, who said it made them "look just like a French whore" or "feel I'm in an old bad Russian movie."[5]

Some retailers pushed back, fearing that their sales would plummet along with hemlines. One midwestern shop owner complained in a letter to *Women's Wear Daily* in mid-August: "You are doing quite a disservice to the manufacturers and retailers by trying to promote a fashion that the customers are not ready for." *Vogue* suffered a 38 percent drop in ad revenue in the first three months of 1971; many of its advertisers had been burned by the backlash. Vreeland was unceremoniously demoted to consulting editor in May, but the damage was already done. Far from selling more dresses, the yo-yoing hemlines eroded consumer confidence in fashion magazines—and the fashion industry in general—and replaced it with a rebellious cynicism.

In spite of the resistance to the midi, the fashion for miniskirts did wane, if only because it became virtually impossible to buy one. The real victor to emerge from the hemline war was . . . pants—which, for many women, provided an attractive and suitably feminist alternative to the much-maligned midi and offered refuge and respite from skirt length debate. As Halston told *The New York Times* in December 1972: "It's all part of women's liberation. Pants give women the freedom to move around they've never had before. They don't have to worry about getting into low furniture or low sports cars. Pants will be with us for many years to come—probably forever if you can make that statement in fashion." His words proved to be prophetic; however, at a time when women in pants were still banned from many restaurants, schools, and offices, pants were not quite as practical as he implied. The midi still had its uses. When Diane von Furstenberg debuted her wildly popular wrap dress (see Chapter 4) the following year, the hemline of the "little bourgeois dress" covered the knee.

But in August 1974, *The New York Times* sounded the death knell for the midi, reporting that "women stayed away in droves, forcing several couture houses and small manufacturers into bankruptcy and the apparel industry into a tailspin." Midi proponent Chester Weinberg's label was one of the casualties. Other retailers reportedly truncated their unsold midis and marketed them as minis. *The Fresno Bee* even printed an obituary: "Dead: The Midi Dress, from Acute Rejection by the American Woman."

The maxi skirt (also known as a "peasant skirt," or "granny dress") continued to enjoy limited popularity. It appealed to hippies, who sought out ethnic and historical styles as an alternative to mainstream fashion, but won widespread acceptance thanks to the tide of historical nostalgia that accompanied the heyday of *Little House on the Prairie*, which aired from 1974 to 1983, and the American bicentennial celebrations of 1976. This glut of Americana may have spurred Ralph Lauren, known for his preppy polo shirts and tailored styles, to launch his cowboy-inspired Ralph Lauren Western and Polo Western lines in 1978. The midi length, virtually absent from high fashion for five years, returned with a vengeance in 1979 in the form of what Lauren dubbed "prairie skirts."

Though prairie skirts recalled midis in length, their look was completely different; instead of awkward, angular A-lines, they were full and flowing, with flounces, ruffles, and scalloped edges. They came in lightweight floral fabrics like calico and chintz, or sometimes rugged denim or leather, with an inch or two of lace or eyelet showing below the hem. They were often paired with a high-necked, puffed-sleeved, bib-fronted shirt, a look *Los Angeles Times* fashion editor Marylou Luther witheringly dismissed as "the little blouse on the prairie." San Francisco–based Gunne Sax and British brand Laura Ashley offered interpretations of the romantic, old-fashioned style that were more affordable than Lauren's, which topped out at $1,000 for a leather version. By the spring of 1982, below-the-knee skirts were outselling pants in New York.[6] But the stronger a trend takes hold, the harder it falls; there is nothing less desirable than last season's must-have fashion. The once-ubiquitous skirt was gone like a tumbleweed by the fall. "The prairie look died last year," a JCPenney publicist admitted in the spring of 1983.[7]

When the modern midi skirt made its first blushing appearance in the Spring/Summer 2014 collections, it similarly brought all the trappings of retro girlishness: flowers, gingham, eyelet, chiffon, pleats, and polka dots. Evoking the swishing petticoats of prom dresses and poodle skirts rather than prairies, it came as a wholesome warm-weather change after a long, bitterly cold winter that saw many Americans held hostage in their homes by a polar vortex. By the fall of 2014, the ladylike midi of the spring collections had taken a more sophisticated, streetwise turn in tweeds, tartans, and jewel-toned satins paired with tall boots and turtlenecks, perhaps with a sliver of skin showing at the waist. Gone were the flowers and polka dots; the new midis were darker and weightier, with a look that was more feminist 1970s than feminine 1950s. And the style stuck; "midi" became a common part of retail taxonomy, and below-the-knee skirts were still being marketed as such in the early 2020s, when "cottagecore" neatly packaged sustainability, handcrafting, and a return to nature in a single nostalgic lifestyle trend.

The hemline war is a distant memory; fashion has laid down its arms. As designer Michael Kors told *Vogue* in May 1992, "the whole direction now is to realize that women . . . have a lot of different moods. Whether you want to feel androgynous and sort of rangy in a trouser and shirt, or very, very romantic in a soft, full skirt at night, or powerful and provocative in a slit, narrow long skirt during the day, or if you just want to fall back on the short, narrow skirt that you've lived in, you can do it." Today, both the industry and its market are too diverse and unwieldy to promote a single silhouette, and if there's anything to be learned from the midi-skirt debacle, it's that women want options, not oracles. Fashion, by definition, depends on novelty; it's not just the essence of fashion but its economic engine. Seasonal trends will always play a role in determining what gets sold and worn. But when it comes to hemlines, it's no longer a question of midi, mini, or maxi; all three can coexist peacefully, along with handkerchief hemlines, high-low hemlines, tulip hemlines, and, of course, pants, in an equally wide array of styles. Even the term "midi" itself has become more elastic, stretching from knee-length to tea-length; there is no uniform midi hemline or shape.

The apotheosis of the midi skirt in the twenty-first century can be attributed to many factors: the popularity of vintage (and vintage-inspired) fashion, fueled by pop culture like *Mad Men* and fin-de-siècle nostalgia; the influence of prominent royal and political women, who combine enviable fashion-ability with diplomatically demure hemlines; and a growing demand for "modest" clothing among conservative Jews and Christians as well as Muslims, the fastest-growing religious group today. Indeed, it's arguable that religious-themed pop culture like HBO's *Big Love* (2006–2011), TLC's reality show *Breaking Amish* (2012–2014), and the Netflix series *Unorthodox* (2020) heralded the return of prairie skirts and dresses, led by designer Batsheva Hay and Stuart Vevers, creative director of Coach. The #MeToo movement, as well, "dramatically changed the way women choose to present themselves," according to Museum of Fine Arts fashion curator Michelle Tolini Finamore. "Being more covered up is okay."[8]

It was not the length of a skirt that made it matronly or

youthful, old-fashioned or trendy, or conservative or progressive. Any skirt could be any of these things, and the only way to win the fashion game was to refuse to play by its rules. In 1971, in the wake of the midi-skirt debacle, the media coined the term "fashion feminist" to describe a woman who dressed to please herself rather than a man, who followed her own inclinations rather than the dictates of Seventh Avenue. "This year," the *Los Angeles Times* predicted, "she'll go to any lengths."

10
THE BODYCON DRESS
Anatomy as Accessory

The bodycon (or body-conscious) dress is hard to define, because it often masquerades as something else: a little black dress, a miniskirt, a naked dress. But, like pornography, you know it when you see it—or don't see it, for the point of the bodycon dress is to call attention to the body rather than the dress itself. The classic bodycon dress is a short, sleeveless shift of skintight, stretchy fabric. It would be demure if not for its doll-like proportions.

Historically, loose (or "slack") clothing was associated with loose morals. The words "sluttish" and "slatternly" originally described careless dress—in either sex—but soon came to signify sexually promiscuous women. Beginning in the seventeenth century, it was a common literary trope that a loose gown could hide an illegitimate pregnancy. Other loose-fitting styles—worn by men and women—were morally suspect simply because they used profligate amounts of fabric, a precious commodity in the preindustrial age. Conversely, from the fifteenth century onward, the disciplining and stiffening of the female body through tight-fitting garments and corsetry—often beginning at a young age—was associated with respectability and self-control. A woman who didn't wear a corset was, literally and figuratively, a "loose" woman.

That began to change in the late nineteenth century as dress reformers led a backlash against uncomfortable and often disfiguring foundation garments like corsets, crinolines, and bustles. In the early twentieth century, fashion designers like Paul Poiret, Mariano Fortuny, and Madeleine Vionnet began to highlight the natural, uncorseted female form rather than an artificially cinched and shaped ideal. Both the pleated Delphos gown and the bias-cut dresses of the 1930s represented attempts to fit clothing to a woman's natural contours, without the benefit of elasticized fabrics (see Chapter 1). Suddenly, tight clothing, not loose clothing, was morally suspect—because it functioned as a second skin, no longer mitigated by an inner layer of stiff foundation garments. As Mae West told costume designer Edith Head: "Make the clothes loose enough to prove I'm a lady, but tight enough to show 'em I'm a woman."[1]

Tight garments made headlines, causing accidents and scandals. In 1908, the couturière Jeanne Margaine-Lacroix sent three mannequins in her "robes-sylphides" (sylph gowns) to the Prix du Prince de Galles race at the Longchamp Racecourse near Paris. It was not unusual for couturiers and their clients to show off new fashions at the horse races. But the "clinging gowns"—apparently worn without corsets—caused a "sensation."

Paul Poiret boasted that he "freed the bust but . . . shackled the legs" with his hobble skirt, introduced in 1910. With as little as twelve inches of fabric in the hem, hobble skirts forced

FIGURE 21. Models wearing form-fitting "Directoire" gowns by Jeanne Margaine-Lacroix caused a scandal at the Longchamp Racecourse in May 1908. (*Chronicle / Alamy Stock Photo*)

women to totter in short steps and made climbing stairs difficult, if not hazardous. They were not just tighter but shorter than previous skirts; shoemakers rejoiced that women's feet were suddenly on display. But others denounced them as "mantraps, or rather womantraps," and complained that they were not only dangerous but ugly.[2] In 1912, New York introduced "stepless" streetcars that allowed women to board without raising their skirts beyond the boundaries of decency.

During the Depression, Hollywood amped up sex and violence to lure filmgoers back to the movies; belly buttons, cleavage, lingerie, and cross-dressing were prevalent on-screen. This prompted a wave of complaints and court cases about on-screen (and off-screen) indecency in the film industry. In response, studios adopted the Motion Picture Production Code, which was fully enforced beginning in 1934. Nicknamed the Hays Code after its enforcer, William H. Hays, chairman of the Motion Picture Producers and Distributors of America, this self-censoring measure prohibited cinematic nudity "in fact or in silhouette" as well as overtly sexual behavior. But studios quickly realized that clinging bias-cut gowns, backless styles, and tight sweaters provided a shortcut around the Hays Code, allowing starlets to show off their figures while leaving their clothes on.

The original "sweater girl" was actress Lana Turner, who made her film debut at sixteen, playing a business school student in 1937's *They Won't Forget*. Although her character had a name, she was murdered twelve minutes into the film, so studio publicists dubbed her "the sweater girl" in reference to her collegiate costume of a tight-fitting sweater, scarf, and beret. ("They had me wear a sweater and walk down the street,"

Turner later told entertainment reporter Bob Thomas. "When you're young . . . they bounce.") A later film, 1942's *Sweater Girl*, was a musical murder mystery set on a college campus, the sweater girl's natural habitat—but in 1941, the Hays Office cracked down on "sweater shots," which violated the Production Code by showing an outline of "intimate parts." The Associated Apparel Manufacturers of Los Angeles protested that "sweaters are wholesome articles of dress and should not be banned by movie censors." When the Hays Code was declared unconstitutional by the Supreme Court in 1952, tight sweaters (and other revealing costumes) returned to the screen.

The "sweater girl" became an American archetype in the 1940s and 1950s, showing off her curves in deceptively demure knitwear. "Miss Sweater Girl" beauty pageants were the midcentury equivalent of wet T-shirt contests. Women without natural assets turned to falsies and other breast augmentation devices that were sold alongside bullet bras and the newly fashionable fluffy sweaters of angora, cashmere, and mohair. Symbols of youth, beauty, and self-conscious sex appeal, sweater girls were alternately praised as paragons of American womanhood and blamed for a spike in sex crimes. "Our real problem is with the bobby-soxers," said Pittsburgh Police Superintendent Harvey J. Scott in 1949. "They are the sweater girls—just kids showing off their curves and apparently liking it. What kind of mothers and wives are they going to be?"[3] Showing off one's curves was bad enough, but liking it? Tight was the new "loose."

Just when it seemed that sweater girls were going the way of the hobble skirt, the full, flowing circle skirts of the postwar period gave way to formfitting sheaths in the 1960s. Instead

FIGURE 22. Lana Turner, the original "sweater girl," was the picture of collegiate chic in *They Won't Forget* (1937). (*Entertainment Pictures / Alamy Stock Photo*)

of shackling the ankles, these "wiggle skirts" and "wiggle dresses" bound the knees, both enforcing and accentuating a halting, hip-swaying gait. New synthetic knits that wouldn't sag (or shrink in the wash) meant that skirts and other garments could be tight-fitting and comfortable at the same time.

The designer jeans of the late 1970s and 1980s were, almost by definition, tight. Ads featured rear views of models with shapely behinds and slogans like: "You know what comes between me and my Calvins? Nothing." Ankle zippers made it possible to pull jeans on over your feet without sacrificing a snug fit. Women (and men) got used to lying down to zip up their jeans, or jumping into a hot bath, fully clothed, to shrink them to fit. In their quest for tighter jeans, designers began incorporating a small amount (1–2 percent) of elastane in their denim. But it wasn't until the early 2000s that "jeggings"—made with up to 6 percent elastane—went on the market, as part of a wider trend for "skinny" pants and leggings. It was no accident that the designer jeans trend coincided with the fitness boom of the 1970s and 1980s. Those with toned butts and thighs wanted to show them off; those without wanted to wear the jeans, so they got in shape.

The association between physical fitness and revealing clothing has a long history. The word "gymnasium" is derived from the Greek "gymnazein," meaning "to exercise naked." The first modern Olympic Games were held in Athens in 1896, inspired by the (nude) athletic contests of ancient Greece. These modern Olympians wore clothes, but, as in ancient times, only men were allowed to compete. International Olympic Committee founder Pierre de Coubertin felt that including women would be "impractical, uninteresting, unaesthetic, and incorrect." It wasn't until 1900 that women were allowed to compete in a very limited number of Olympic sports.

When Jack LaLanne opened the first American health club in 1939, many doctors still advised *against* rigorous exercise. LaLanne encouraged women to try weight lifting, but few did; fitness culture remained overwhelmingly male. That began to change in 1961, when President John F. Kennedy—who lettered in swimming at Harvard—launched the U.S. Physical Fitness Program, framing fitness as essential to children's health and the country's military preparedness. In the period of unprecedented prosperity that followed World War II, Americans had, literally, gone soft. Kennedy's curriculum dramatically improved physical education in American schools, training a new generation of athletes of both sexes. American runner Frank Shorter's victory in the 1972 Olympic marathon inspired a craze for recreational running, or "jogging," while the passage of Title IX in the same year opened up athletic opportunities for female students, especially in cross-country and track. Outdoor "fitness trails" appeared in public parks. President Gerald Ford—a former college football hero and avid skier—built a pool and a home gym in the White House.

The documentary *Pumping Iron,* released in 1977, made celebrities of competitive bodybuilders Arnold Schwarzenegger and Lou Ferrigno. The 1985 sequel, *Pumping Iron II: The Women,* featured four female bodybuilders, but its bikini-clad contestants divided audiences and the on-screen judges, who associated bulging muscles with masculinity. Women were more drawn to a new fitness fad: aerobics. Developed by the military to train recruits in the 1960s, aerobic exercise went mainstream when Jane Fonda released her first workout video (on VHS and Betamax) in 1982. Fitness was becoming big business, selling not just videos but leg warmers and leotards, high-tech sneakers, diet books, and home exercise devices like stationary bicycles, resistance bands, and the Thighmaster, invented by a Swedish physical therapist. (Plastic surgery was booming, too.) Gyms had once meant rusty weights and a boxing ring; now, luxury, members-only, twenty-four-hour "fitness centers" were opening all over the world, equipped with racquetball courts, therapy pools, and high-tech exercise machines that allowed patrons to lift weights without a spotter. Fully loaded home gyms followed. After massive growth in the 1970s, recreational tennis peaked in popularity in the 1980s. As women became physically fitter and stronger, they became more comfortable in their own skin, regardless of what they were wearing.

Fitness culture invaded pop culture. A headband-wearing Olivia Newton-John sang while doing leg lifts and jumping jacks in her video for "Physical," the earworm of 1981. The 1985 movie *Perfect* was a romance between a *Rolling Stone* reporter (John Travolta) researching fitness culture and an aerobics instructor (Jamie Lee Curtis). Hit films of the era celebrated running (*Chariots of Fire*), rowing (*Oxford Blues*), bicycling (*Breaking Away, American Flyers, Quicksilver*), boxing (*Raging Bull*, the *Rocky* movies), martial arts (*The Karate Kid, Bloodsport, Kickboxer*), ice hockey (*Youngblood*), and wrestling (*Vision Quest*) as well as baseball, basketball, and football. Schwarzenegger and Ferrigno parlayed their bodybuilding fame into beefcake acting careers. There was even an aerobics-themed horror movie, 1987's *Aerobicide*.

Fashion photography, too, began to worship the cult of the body. Helmut Newton, Bruce Weber, and Herb Ritts produced ads and magazine spreads featuring NSFW images of flawless male and female physiques, prompting *New York Times* critic Hilton Kramer to complain in 1975: "Fashion itself has now become a subdivision of pornographic culture." Calvin Klein and other designers discovered that naked bodies could sell clothes and perfume. Klein's sexually provocative jeans commercials featuring fifteen-year-old Brooke Shields (shot by Richard Avedon) were banned by ABC and CBS in 1980. In the early 1990s, his underwear ad campaign (shot by Herb Ritts) featured a nearly nude Kate Moss and Mark Wahlberg, amid contemporaneous controversies over nudity in ads for Yves Saint Laurent, Gucci, Tom Ford, and the Wonderbra. By that time, digital retouching had become commonplace in fashion photography, creating bodies that were both idealized and hyperrealistic.

Increasingly, a woman's most important fashion accessory was a slim, toned body. As James Galanos diplomatically explained in 1973: "There are two kinds of ladies: the fashionable ones who keep their figures trim so they can get into the new things that come along, and those who depend on undergarments."[4] But traditional shaping garments like corsets and girdles were becoming harder and harder to conceal under the formfitting, skin-showing fashions of the time. As the fitness craze took off, the fashion for body-conscious and body-baring clothing followed; women who had once depended on undergarments for a perfect physique increasingly found that they had nothing to wear. "Clothes no longer shaped the body, as they had through the stiff-fabric designs and industrial-strength undergarments of prior decades," *Vogue* editor in chief Grace Mirabella remembered in her memoir, *In and Out of Vogue*. "Now, the body gave shape to clothes, and the result was pure gutsiness, sheer ease, and thoroughly modern beauty."

Just as aerobics and Jazzercise battled for supremacy in the 1980s, two designers fought for the title of "King of Cling": Azzedine Alaïa and Hervé Léger. In 1989, they both introduced short, sleeveless dresses constructed of heavily elasticized bands. It was a new twist on the wrap dress, suggesting not liberation but bondage. Alaïa called his version the "mummy" dress, evoking ancient Egyptian tomb wrappings; Léger's was the "bandage" dress. The spiral line was nothing new; Charles James and Jeanne Paquin had experimented with it in the 1930s, and Halston in the 1970s, but to much different effect. What was different: the construction—rows of concentric circles rather than a single piece of fabric sewn in a spiral—and the elasticized materials. "Imagine an ACE bandage wrapped mummy-like, with a very high hemline and plunging décolletage, and you've got the idea," the *Los Angeles Times* said. "It's fashion first aid, but not for the fainthearted."

If the sinuous spiral-cut gowns of the 1930s and 1970s revealed the female form by creating cling in fabrics that had none, the bandage shaped the body; it was more corset than cocoon. Alaïa and Léger discovered a third rail of dressmaking: instead of cutting or draping, they molded strips of fabric to the figure, taking advantage of new and improved stretch fabrics previously reserved for undergarments and workout wear. Both designers had trained as sculptors. Alaïa had studied at the Institute of Fine Arts in Tunis, where he was born, making clothes on the side to pay for his art supplies. He built up his dresses in the way a sculptor builds up clay, layer by layer. His barely-there dresses used as many as forty-three tiny scraps of fabric, pieced together to encase the wearer's contours, so the woven cloth would hold the body like a knit.[5] "When I start to design, I think about the shoulders, the waist, the bust," he said. "I think about the woman and how I can make her more beautiful. Beautiful and strong. A woman must be strong on the same level as a man. Men and women have the same minds. They must have the same strength."[6]

It was a philosophy Alaïa and Léger shared with a trio of enfants terribles who started designing around the same time and for the same type of woman: Thierry Mugler, Claude Montana, and Jean-Paul Gaultier. Although each had his own distinct vision, all three imagined a new way of dressing that showcased the 1980s woman's newfound power, with dramatically padded shoulders, uplifted busts, cinched waists, and endless legs. They took former fetish items—lingerie, leather, latex —and made them fashion. In 1989, Mugler discovered corset maker and wearer Mr. Pearl, launching a collaboration that was still going strong in 2019, when Kim Kardashian wore a Mr. Pearl corset under a Mugler latex dress at the Met Gala (see Chapter 7). Their futuristic silhouettes exaggerated femininity almost to the point of parody, with cone-shaped bras and motorcycle-shaped bustiers. These were superhero costumes for a new breed of superwomen, modeled by statuesque "supermodels." While famous beauties had once been identified by their outstanding body parts (see Chapter 7), it was increasingly difficult to single out one superlative feature. In 1989, *Time* dubbed frequent *Sports Illustrated* swimsuit issue cover girl Elle Macpherson "The Body." It was a fitting moniker for an era in which women were supposedly—to quote the title of *Cosmopolitan* editor in chief Helen Gurley Brown's 1982 book—*Having It All*.

If the bodycon dress was a skintight superhero costume, its civilian alter ego was the power suit, office attire for a new breed of working women who had white-collar careers and college educations. Though it had masculine styling and details like pinstripes, flap pockets, or notched lapels, the stereotypical power suit was a brightly colored skirt suit—and often a short, tight skirt at that, equipped with a slit for ease of movement. "The traditional business uniform of men . . . continues in favor not only because of conservatism but because it is eminently practical," Kennedy Fraser observed in 1979. "It is a style of dress that can be forgotten about while the people wearing it devote their attention to the job in hand." Adapted for women, however, the man's suit "gains triviality and becomes something like a costume for a role," Fraser complained. "Many of the new fashions for young executive women somehow imply a playing at careerism."[7] Unlike its practical, anonymous masculine counterpart, the eye-catching power suit demanded to be the center of attention; moussed hair, shoulder pads, and high heels physically enlarged its wearer. Instead of a successful woman, it suggested an *unsuccessful* imitation of a man. The bodycon dress, by contrast, was all sleek curves and long limbs. It translated women's newfound socioeconomic power into an unmistakably feminine idiom.

Alaïa launched his label in 1980, after working for Guy Laroche and Thierry Mugler, who encouraged him to go solo. But he was virtually unknown outside of Paris when he was asked to costume Grace Jones to play the villain in the 1985 James Bond film *A View to a Kill* (see Plate 17). Her slinky hooded dresses, thong bodysuits, black leather, and pinstriped wool jackets with aggressive shoulder pads got attention, but not necessarily the right kind. Jill Gerson of the Knight Ridder News Service veered perilously close to slut-shaming when she wrote: "There is a certain kind of woman—Tina Turner, Raquel Welch, Paloma Picasso—who likes her clothes tight, very tight so that they caress every curve, hugging the waist and cupping the derriere. For that certain kind of woman, here is a certain kind of designer: Azzedine Alaïa."[8] But other critics appreciated his naughty-but-nice aesthetic. "Because of Alaïa's technical skill and his eye for proportion, his clothes were never tawdry," wrote *The Washington Post*'s Robin Givhan. "Instead, they were masterful." In October 1985, Jones and model Iman would wear early iterations of the mummy dress to the French "Oscars de la Mode," where Alaïa was named Best Designer of the Year.

It was a very different film that would make him a household name, however. A red Alaïa mummy dress plays a pivotal role in the 1995 movie *Clueless*; the heroine, Beverly Hills high schooler Cher Horowitz, is held up at gunpoint on her way home from a Christmas party and made to lie down in a liquor store parking lot. When Amy Heckerling wrote the screenplay, she didn't know who the "totally important designer" Cher was wearing would be; costume designer Mona May found the lipstick-red mummy dress and it was written into the script. "You don't understand, this is an Alaïa!" Cher protests. "Nobody really knew who Alaïa was before," remembered May—much less how to pronounce his name. At a time when teenagers were going grunge, the movie was an unapologetic celebration of high fashion. When Gaultier costumed 1997's sci-fi film *The Fifth Element*, he paid a winking tribute to his friend Alaïa; the heroine, played by model Milla Jovovich, is the product of a Frankenstein-like regeneration experiment. She begins the movie strapped down by medical bandages and breaks free of them, leaving her clad in a revealing jumpsuit composed of white bandage strips.

Alaïa's models were glamazons: confident, complicated, and somewhat intimidating, especially when photographed next to the five-foot-nothing designer. "I make clothes," Alaïa once declared. "Women make fashion." Naomi Campbell was his longtime muse; early clients included Cher, Diana Ross, and Madonna. In addition to his mummy bandages, Alaïa celebrated the female form in sweaterdresses, bodysuits, and "moiré acetate gowns so tight the models had to mince down the runway."[9] Alaïa could be complicated and intimidating himself, cultivating a reputation as a maverick who refused to play by the fashion system's rules. He presented his collections on his own schedule, when he felt ready, in his apartment, rather than conforming to the Fashion Week calendar. In 1983, Alaïa barred a photographer from his show because he didn't approve of the way his paper had sized its photos of his last collection; he was known to reduce fashion editors to tears over coverage he disliked. Bloomingdale's buyers stopped coming to his shows after he squabbled with the department store over the way they presented his clothes.[10] If Léger often gets credit for inventing the bandage dress, it is likely because Alaïa offended Anna Wintour and got himself exiled from the pages of *Vogue*. In 1987, *Women's Wear Daily* declared the volatile designer "finished" after a feud with publisher John Fairchild.[11] But he was just getting started.

Up to his death in 2017, Alaïa maintained that his mummy dress had preceded Léger's bandage dress, and photographic evidence supports him. (He also accused Roberto Cavalli of copying his work.) But Léger had worked for Alaïa, and he gave the bandage dress its own unique origin story. After dropping out of art school to become a hairstylist, Léger worked as a milliner. "One day in a factory I found some bands that were headed for the garbage," he explained. "They gave me the idea of taking those bands and putting them next to one another as one does making a hat."[12] Karl Lagerfeld recruited him to Fendi and encouraged him to change his surname from the difficult-to-pronounce Peugnet to Léger (which is reminiscent of "légèreté," the French word for "lightness" or "frivolity"). Léger designed banded fur skirts for Fendi in the early 1980s. He opened his own boutique in Paris in 1985, but it closed due to financial problems in 1989. A few months later, he debuted his stretch viscose bandage dress and turned his career around.

"My dresses are designed for women who are at ease with their bodies," Léger told *Vogue* in March 1992—though he hastened to add that he had clients as old as fifty and some who were "quite *plump*." He even made a bandage wedding gown for Iman to wear when she married David Bowie in 1992. Léger was especially popular in Los Angeles, where the Beverly Hills branch of Neiman Marcus sold more Léger than any other store in the chain. Famous fans included Nicole Kidman, Geena Davis, and Cindy Crawford, who has said on Instagram that Léger's dresses "held you in all the right places" (see Plate 18). Rather than showing figure flaws, fans argued, Léger's clothes corrected them, sucking everything in. Léger produced about 1,000 handmade bandage dresses per year, alongside other types of bodycon garments.

It wasn't enough; in 1998, Léger sold his company to the Los Angeles–based BCBG Max Azria Group. At first, the partnership was amicable, but when Léger feuded with the new owners in 1999, he was fired and lost the rights to his name and his signature bandage dresses. Max Azria relaunched the style in 2007, without its creator. "I didn't want to launch until I truly understood the whole idea," explained chief creative officer Lubov Azria. "A bandage dress isn't woven, it's all knitted on a knitting machine and is a completely different concept. People assume it's cut-and-sew, but there's no cutting. It's knitted in a panel and then attached."[13] While Léger had used only one width of bandage, Azria experimented with thinner ones. A new generation of clients—Kim Kardashian, Victoria Beckham, Rihanna, Jennifer Lopez—took notice, and Léger bandage dresses, new and vintage, became a fixture of the red carpet again, along with homages by Christopher Kane, Proenza Schouler, Roberto Cavalli, and Olivier Rousteing for Balmain. Léger—having changed his name once more, to Hervé Leroux—briefly became creative director of Guy Laroche, where Alaïa had once worked, creating Hilary Swank's backless bodycon gown for the 2005 Oscars. He died on October 4, 2017; Alaïa (who was seventeen years older) followed just over a month later. In the same year, BCBG Max Azria Group filed for bankruptcy and the Hervé Léger label was acquired by the fashion and media conglomerate Authentic Brands Group.

If wearing tight clothes once ran the risk of moral shaming, women who wear them today—in a Peloton-powered culture no less obsessed with fitness (or at least thinness) than it was in the 1980s—risk being shamed for having imperfect figures, raising questions about who "gets" to wear bodycon styles. "The pursuit of slimness is one of the chief labors of the modern woman," British *Vogue* noted in 1922—an observation that held true for much of the twentieth century. That began to change as "fat acceptance" and "fat activism" gained traction in the late 1960s and early 1970s, in tandem with (and often overlapping with) second-wave feminism and the civil rights movement. In 1968, feminists disrupted the Miss America pageant in Atlantic City, dumping bras, girdles, curlers, false eyelashes, wigs, and women's magazines into a "Freedom Trash Can" to protest paternalistic ideals of beauty. As more women forged new paths in the workplace, politics, and higher education, they prioritized social transformation over the frivolous dictates of fashion and anticipated better living through technology. In 1967, *Vogue* editor Diana Vreeland predicted: "In the year 2001 so many physical problems will have been surmounted that a woman's beauty will be a dream that will be completely obtainable."[14]

One wonders if Vreeland prophesied the invention of Spanx. Launched in 2000 by entrepreneur Sara Blakely, Spanx sold shapewear that you could actually wear under bodycon clothing. The pieces weren't revolutionary—footless control-top pantyhose, spandex bicycle shorts, nude bodysuits—and they weren't cheap. But they used comfortable, easily camouflaged modern materials and had cute names like "Power Panties" and "Bra-Cha-Cha." Just as importantly, they espoused an up-front, empowering attitude toward something that was formerly unmentionable: figure flaws. Blakely realized that most women in America wore size 14 and up, and many of them wanted to wear bodycon dresses, too. Even thin women (even famous women!) freely admitted to wearing Spanx to smooth out lumps and bumps—much like a bandage dress. Blakely chose the name Spanx for its "virgin-whore tension," a recurring feature of bodycon clothes, with the shifting meanings of "loose."[15]

The problem of body-shaming—and the solution to it—was further transformed by social media, which forced a public reckoning with the unrealistic beauty standards historically promoted by sexist (and often ableist, ageist, and racist) media and culture. In recent years, the term "body positivity" has been used to denote acceptance of bodies of all shapes, sizes, and colors—whether your own body or those of others. It acknowledges that beauty—once virtually synonymous with thinness and whiteness in fashion media and marketing—now takes many forms. It encompasses a more nuanced understanding of disordered eating and the physical and psychological dangers of excessive dieting and exercise. It recognizes that strength and femininity are not mutually exclusive. It celebrates images of ordinary women and plus-size influencers with hashtags like #honormycurves and #effyourbeautystandards. It has prominent celebrity supporters: Lizzo, Demi Lovato, Serena Williams, and Ashley Graham among them. Within the fashion industry, body positivity means offering inclusive sizing, using unretouched photos, and employing models (and mannequins) of varying sizes, races, ages, and abilities. Halfway between self-care and social justice, body positivity encourages women (and men, too) to wear tight, revealing, or sexy clothes regardless of their body type, without fear of fat-shaming or slut-shaming. "You've got to love your body," Léger advised his clients in 1994.[16] The fashion industry is beginning to realize that love is one size fits all.

CONCLUSION

The Future of Skirts

A re dresses doomed? In 2008, Hillary Clinton ran for president of the United States. Though hardly the first woman to run for America's highest office, she was the first to be a front-runner, and her wardrobe attracted as much scrutiny as her policies. Clinton's trademark pantsuits became a late-night punch line and a symbol of her somewhat stereotypical embodiment of second-wave feminism. But they were also a powerful form of political propaganda and personal branding, telegraphing her transition from skirted First Lady to suited candidate, and encouraging voters to take the New York senator seriously as a potential president. When she conceded the Democratic nomination to Barack Obama, the eventual winner, she invoked the familiar metaphor of the glass ceiling, representing the invisible barriers that keep women from rising to positions of power, telling her supporters: "Although we weren't able to shatter that highest, hardest glass ceiling this time, thanks to you, it's got about eighteen million cracks in it, and the light is shining through like never before, filling us all with the hope and the sure knowledge that the path will be a little easier next time."

It was. In 2016, Clinton ran again and won the Democratic nomination thanks to "Pantsuit Nation"—an informal coalition of women united under the banner of Clinton's preferred campaign garb. Although she lost the Electoral College and the presidency to Donald Trump, she won the popular vote, and her pantsuits paved the way for an unprecedented number of women to enter the presidential race in the 2020 election cycle. One of them, fellow pantsuit aficionado Kamala Harris, became America's first female vice president. The glass ceiling, although not quite shattered, is flimsier than ever.

But even as Clinton was making her historic ascent from First Lady to senator to presidential hopeful, a different and disturbing obstacle to women's advancement was rising: the glass staircase. The brainchild of Apple CEO Steve Jobs, this architectural marvel formed the centerpiece of the first Apple store in New York, which opened in SoHo in 2002. "We had a two-story space, which is a great challenge to get people to go up or down," architect Peter Bohlin explained. "So we thought of glass. . . . We made these stairs that were quite ethereal."[1] Not only were the treads made of clouded glass, but they "floated," with open gaps in place of risers. The see-through stairs enticed shoppers to the upper level and made the historic building—a former post office built in 1920—look not only modern but futuristic. The Instagram-friendly feature would become a hallmark of Apple's retail stores; the three-story spiral version in its Meatpacking District branch, which opened in 2007, was hailed as the largest and most complex glass staircase ever built at the time.

This widely touted feat of engineering was also a textbook example of gender bias in design—and in the fast-growing tech industry itself. "If I were commissioning the interior of any kind of store and someone brought me blueprints including glass staircases, I'd tell him to take a hike," technology blogger Joanne McNeil noted. "If he's not intuitive enough to grasp that women in skirts will be uncomfortable walking upstairs, clouded glass or not, then what other errors has he made in his design?"[2] In a talk on closing the gender gap in tech at the 2014 Above All Human conference, software engineer and diversity advocate Tracy Chou told the audience: "When I first saw the glass staircases in an Apple Store, my very first thought was that there must have been few women working there, because I didn't want to walk up those stairs in a skirt."[3] And web developer Nicole Sullivan blogged after a visit to an Apple store: "Did anyone sit down and say, 'I'm going to make it impossible for women (and men in kilts) to get to the Genius Bar'? Of course not. . . . But does that change the fact that women may find it much more difficult to get to their Genius Bar appointments (or their job at the Genius Bar)? No."[4]

Los Angeles Times culture columnist Carolina A. Miranda went on to cite other examples of public buildings with transparent stairs, elevated walkways, and upper-level floors—including, most troublingly, architecture schools. "This not only affects the women who work and study in those buildings . . . but it normalizes the idea among architecture students that transparent walkways are just a benign architectural feature," she wrote. "They are not." In 2011, a female judged slammed the $105 million new courthouse in Franklin County, Ohio, for using clear glass risers between the thin concrete treads that formed its airy staircase. "I wear dresses because that's my personal choice," Judge Julie M. Lynch told 10TV News. "When you stand under the stairwell, you can see right up through them. . . . How can you open a brand-new building and not take in consideration half the population?" The Associated Press reported: "Security guards have been instructed to watch for people craning their necks."[5]

By a grim coincidence, 2002—the year Apple's SoHo store opened—was also the year that cell phones equipped with cameras went on the market, leading to another unwelcome phenomenon for skirt wearers: the upskirt photo. "Upskirting"—surreptitiously looking up a woman's skirt for the purpose of sexual gratification—has a history almost as long as that of skirts themselves, though the term emerged more recently, with the advent of the digital camera. The practice was especially pernicious in the eighteenth and nineteenth centuries, when women wore stiff hoop petticoats and crinolines with "drawers"—drawstring underpants open at the crotch—or no underpants at all. (Ironically, underpants were considered racy, as pants were an exclusively male garment.) Jean-Honoré Fragonard's iconic 1767 painting *The Swing* celebrates the simple pleasures of childhood games alongside the more adult pleasures of upskirting. The cancan—a high-kicking dance performed in French music halls of the Belle Époque—derived its appeal and notoriety from the fact that the dancers wore drawers. Accidental upskirting—thanks to a fall or a wardrobe malfunction—was the stuff of pornographic prints and bawdy poetry. As art historian Anne Hollander observed, "being able to see up a woman's skirt—so long and voluminous for so many centuries—must have been a masculine, if not an artistic, preoccupation of long standing. . . . The sight of the nude leg undoubtedly carried rather intense associations with undefended nudity higher up."[6]

By the close of the twentieth century, this violation was compounded by the digital camera's ability to preserve and disseminate upskirt views. Victims of upskirt photographs found that the new technology was often not covered by existing voyeurism or public decency laws, triggering a flurry of new legislation and rules banning cell phones from gyms, locker rooms, and public restrooms. But women (and girls) were vulnerable to upskirt photos virtually everywhere: in crowds, on public transportation, in restaurants, at school, and, especially, on staircases, glass or otherwise. In 2012, Apple's Hong Kong store was blacklisted by the region's biggest political party as a haven for Peeping Toms who lurked under its glass staircase, iPhones in hand. When Apple remodeled its twenty-four-hour Fifth Avenue flagship in 2017, the glass staircase was replaced with one made of stainless steel. At a time when dresses were more popular than they'd been in decades, however, the gesture seemed like a baby step toward rectifying an insidious and persistent form of discrimination, which is all the more odious because it does not necessarily target women but simply overlooks their existence.

In retrospect, the influx of women's pants and pantsuits into the workplace—and every other place—in the 1970s, 1980s, and 1990s may be remembered as a blip, or perhaps a failed experiment. More likely, we will remember the popularity of pants as an important but temporary transitional era, ushering women into male-dominated workplaces and other corridors of power. Pantsuit Nation notwithstanding, the early twenty-first century saw a dress renaissance led by prominent and influential women like Kate Middleton, who became Duchess of Cambridge in 2011; Michelle Obama, First Lady of the United States from 2009 to 2017; and Marissa Mayer, the Google VP who became CEO of Yahoo! in 2012. According to *New York Times* fashion critic Vanessa Friedman, these women "helped open up a sense of what women can wear as they start to feel more comfortable in their own power positions."[7] For Clinton and many women of her generation, power meant wearing the pants, both literally and metaphorically, by inserting themselves into historically masculine spaces and spheres. That accomplished, women pursued a different kind of liberation: the freedom to wear whatever they wanted.

After leaving the White House, Michelle Obama famously joked about her husband: "People take pictures of the shoes I wear, the bracelets, the necklace—they didn't comment that for eight years he wore that same tux." Women in the public eye cannot retreat into the sober anonymity of a suit and tie. As First Lady, Obama used her time under the microscope thoughtfully, promoting young American fashion talent—particularly immigrants and designers of color like Jason Wu, who made both of her inaugural gowns (see Chapter 1). She mixed high-end, directional pieces with mass-market labels and occasionally swapped skirts for pants, jeans, capris, and, once, a controversial pair of shorts. But the image she left behind for posterity—her official portrait by Amy Sherald—may be Obama's most powerful fashion statement. The composition is dominated by the long skirt of her Milly halter gown, a colorful geometric print simultaneously evoking her husband's campaign logo, with its stylized sunrise and amber waves of grain; the strikingly modernist quilts created by Black women in Gee's Bend, Alabama; and the stars and stripes of the American flag, with Obama sitting in for Betsy Ross. The cascading skirt also recalled presidential candidate Jesse Jackson's speech at the 1984 Democratic National Convention, in which he compared America to a quilt: "Many patches, many pieces, many colors, many sizes, all woven and held together by a common thread." While some critics felt that the portrait was not a good likeness of Obama, its chic synthesis of tradition and modernity, patriotism and progressivism, was instantly recognizable.

If Obama's gown expressed unity, another dress worn by a notable Democrat—Congresswoman Stacey Plaskett—projected partisan strength. In 2021, Plaskett won praise from political pundits and style gurus alike when she deftly prosecuted Donald Trump's second impeachment wearing a showstopping midi dress in Democratic blue, paired with high heels that added inches to her already statuesque six-foot frame (see Plate 19). Social media posts compared her to a superhero defending America's democracy. Her clothing didn't overshadow her fierce performance; it underlined and enhanced it. Plaskett proved that you don't have to wear a pantsuit or "power suit" to project power—a message that resonated especially with younger women, who could not remember a time when wearing pants was a controversial right to be won. The dress was not just a bold color but formfitting. As Plaskett told *Elle:* "That was very intentional." So were the cape-like long sleeves, which were slit to expose Plaskett's bare arms as she moved. "It was a way of subtly thumbing my nose at the dress code because women have been told they can't wear sleeveless dresses," she explained; sleeveless dresses were banned from the floor of the House of Representatives until 2017. Showing some skin was also Plaskett's way of owning the fact that she "was the only Black woman in that room."[8]

Fashion is uniquely qualified to capture and capitalize on intersectionality—the interconnection of class, race, and gender. As Costume Institute curator Andrew Bolton noted in 2021, "there's no art form that addresses the politics of identity more than fashion." Just a few months after Plaskett's bravura turn in blue, Interior Secretary Deb Haaland—the first Native American Cabinet secretary in U.S. history—made a similar statement when she was sworn in wearing a long, colorful ribbon skirt, a traditional Pueblo garment laden with celebratory symbolism. Haaland ended up on the August 2021 cover of *InStyle* magazine, wearing her own Native clothing, under the headline "Badass Women." These watershed moments suggested that society has progressed beyond that idea that women have to dress like men to compete with them; pants are an option, but they're not the only option.

And they're not necessarily the best option: multiple studies have shown that women who work with conservative men (whether politicians or plumbers) are more likely to win their respect if they wear skirts and other conventionally feminine garments. "Blue-collar men react negatively to women wearing pants," John T. Molloy wrote in the 2008 edition of *New Women's Dress for Success*. As former British Prime Minister Margaret Thatcher chided a female press secretary at the Conservative Party's 2000 conference: "Never trousers, my dear. They rob a woman of her authority."[9]

Pants are no longer the only option for men, either. In fashion, terms like "androgynous" and "unisex" have historically been applied to traditionally male garments that are adopted by women, and rarely the reverse. But that has changed in recent years, alongside evolving social, psychological, and medical conceptions of gender. The #MeToo movement that went viral in 2017 brought a backlash against culturally ingrained tolerance of sexual assault and harassment and confronted the effects of "toxic masculinity"—a stereotypical view of manhood that harms both men and women. High-profile nonbinary, genderfluid, and transgender celebrities like Elliot Page, Billie Eilish, Caitlyn Jenner, and Laverne Cox have redefined red carpet fashion, even as transgender rights and "bathroom laws" remain political hot buttons in the United States. In the fashion industry, the more flexible and open-ended terms "gender-neutral" and "gender-inclusive" have replaced the monolithic "unisex." This semantic shift has not only affected branding and marketing but has extended to androgynous and transgender fashion models and fashion influencers such as Andreja Pejić, Laith Ashley, Erika Linder, Leyna Bloom, and Harmony Boucher.

Men have worn skirts in many cultures for a long time and continue to do so, including the kilt, dhoti, sarong, djellaba, and taʻovala, the wrapped mat memorably modeled by Pita Taufatofua, Tonga's flag bearer at the 2016, 2018, and 2020 Olympics (see Plate 20). (Also in 2016, Disney's animated film *Moana* dressed Hawaiian demigod Maui—voiced by Dwayne Johnson, an actor of Samoan descent—in a ti leaf skirt.) Indeed, just as women have worn pants in many non-Western cultures over many centuries without controversy, men have been wearing skirts a lot longer than they've been wearing pants, which were first adopted as an equestrian garment in Asia and not widely embraced in Europe until the late Middle

Ages. The skirted robes still worn by clergymen, judges, and academics are vestiges of what was once everyday menswear; their continued use centuries later speaks to the respect accorded these offices. Part of the reason men's skirts are more visible and accepted today is a resurgence in national and ethnic pride amid rapid globalization, expressed by wearing traditional or regional garments.

These male skirts cannot be confused with drag, a performance of gender identity that has existed in various forms for centuries but is today most closely associated with New York's ballroom scene. Once an underground phenomenon, the flamboyant, fashion-conscious gay subculture went mainstream in films like *The Adventures of Priscilla, Queen of the Desert* (1994), *To Wong Foo, Thanks for Everything! Julie Newmar* (1995), and *The Birdcage* (1996), and in television shows like *RuPaul's Drag Race* (2009) and *Pose* (2018). When Thomas Neuwirth—the drag artist who performs as Conchita Wurst—won the 2014 Eurovision Song Contest in a sparkly gown *and* a full beard, drag's ascendancy was complete. Though beards had been part of drag since the 1970s, Wurst's beard—seen by 195 million viewers worldwide—touched a nerve. Neuwirth told Reuters that the beard was "a statement to say that you can achieve anything, no matter who you are or how you look." Fans and supporters donned fake beards in tribute to Wurst, but critics called it a beard too far. In Russia, antigay men shaved their own beards as part of a social media protest. Irish broadcaster Terry Wogan came under fire for describing the contest as a "freak show," with Wurst as the Bearded Lady.

In retrospect, Wurst's beard was a harbinger of a growing hunger for clothes that are neither traditional men's skirts nor drag but feminine garments, worn as a form of fashion and self-expression rather than female impersonation. Like so many provocative fashion trends, this one may have originated in the music industry as a reaction against the macho culture of traditional rock music. Glam rockers like David Bowie, Marc Bolan, Iggy Pop, and Elton John gleefully experimented with androgyny in the 1970s, including wearing makeup and skirts; the New Romantics followed suit in the 1980s. But there was no suggestion of androgyny when Kurt Cobain appeared on the cover of the September 1993 issue of the British magazine *The Face* wearing a floral dress—a look he and his Nirvana bandmates had worn onstage and in their videos (see Plate 21). This was, transparently, a man in a woman's dress. He may have been wearing dark eyeliner, but he also wore a goatee and a man's white undershirt. It was the stark contrast between his male and female attributes, rather than the artful blurring of boundaries, that made the image compelling and controversial.

"Wearing a dress shows I can be as feminine as I want," Cobain explained to the *Los Angeles Times* in August 1993. "I'm a heterosexual . . . big deal. But if I was a homosexual, it wouldn't matter either." Cobain's sexuality was not in question; he was, famously, married to Courtney Love at the time and often borrowed her trademark baby doll dresses. He also occasionally donned feather boas, Jackie O sunglasses, and leopard-print coats. As he told *Melody Maker* in December 1992, "I like to wear dresses because they're comfortable. If I said we do it to be subversive then that would be a load of shit, because men in bands wearing dresses isn't controversial anymore."

Indeed, many male grunge artists—including the Lemonheads and the Smashing Pumpkins—mixed dresses with overtly butch sartorial signifiers like tattoos, flannel "lumberjack" shirts, thermal underwear, and work boots. The look was androgynous only in the sense that women, too, wore similar assemblages of floral frocks, flannel shirts, and heavy boots within the grunge subculture. This iconoclasm was partly born of the grunge ethos of DIY anti-capitalism—assembling vintage and secondhand clothes from thrift shops, flea markets, and military surplus shops—and the damp, outdoorsy environment of the Pacific Northwest, where the "Seattle sound" was born. (In the late 1990s, Seattle construction worker Steven "Krash" Villegas cut up a pair of army surplus pants to make himself a washable skirt with pockets that he could wear while working on his motorcycle; he started selling them at Pike Place Market, and founded the Utilikilts label in 2000.) But fashion journalist Joshua Sims detected a larger social phenomenon at work: Cobain, like many of his contemporaries in Generation X, had grown up with a working mother and no father figure.[10] His dresses questioned the role and value of traditional masculinity, balancing gender confusion with gender confidence. As Iggy Pop has said: "I'm not ashamed to dress 'like a woman' because I don't think it's shameful to be a woman."

Fashion designers have long experimented with gender in their own wardrobes; think of Chanel with her "beach pyjamas" and matelots, or Jean Paul Gaultier and Alexander McQueen with their kilts. Marc Jacobs, whose Spring 1993 collection for Perry Ellis was inspired by grunge, incorporated kilts into his wardrobe before branching out into skirts in traditionally feminine styles and fabrics. In 2012, he wore a black lace Comme des Garçons Homme Plus shirtdress over white boxer shorts to the Met Ball, as an alternative to what he called a "boring" tuxedo (and, possibly, as a callout to his friend Kate Moss's iconic naked dress; see Chapter 7). As the designer told *New York* magazine: "I bought . . . one, and I discovered how nice it felt to wear. They're comfortable, and wearing it made me happy, so I bought more. And now I just can't stop wearing them."

From the short-lived *Star Trek* "skant" and sporadic appearances on the runway in menswear shows—calculated to generate Fashion Week headlines more than retail sales—men's skirts have claimed a more prominent presence in fashion and popular culture. Actors Jared Leto and Oscar Isaac have worn them on the red carpet. Actor-musician Jaden Smith wore a Louis Vuitton skirt in the designer's Spring/Summer 2016 womenswear ad campaign. "He's not a man in transition . . . or a man wearing clothing that looks as if it could be worn by either gender," *New York Times* fashion critic Vanessa Friedman said. "He is a man who happens to be wearing obviously female clothes. And while he doesn't look like a girl in them, he actually looks pretty good." In 2018, nonbinary *Queer Eye* cast member Jonathan Van Ness began wearing dresses—along with heels, purses, and his usual long hair and full beard—on the show and to promotional events; he even rocked a Maison Margiela naked dress on the red carpet at the Creative Arts Emmys (see Chapter 7). While kilts continued to gain acceptance—often in nontraditional, ultramasculine materials like black leather and camouflage—they increasingly shared retail and red-carpet space with more feminine-looking men's skirts.

On February 15, 2019, after a week of fall menswear shows in New York, *GQ*'s website confidently predicted: "2019 Is the Year Men Will Start Wearing Skirts." Days later, *Pose* actor Billy Porter proved them right, arriving at the Oscars wearing an ensemble designed for him by Christian Siriano: a black velvet tuxedo jacket and white shirt paired with a strapless black velvet gown (see Plate 22). "I'm an activist," he explained. "I knew that that tuxedo gown at the Oscars would create a conversation surrounding what gender means, what all these rules we put on everybody in life. We've gotten past a problem with women wearing pants. When women wear pants it's powerful. When men wear a dress it's disgusting. We're not doing that anymore. I'm not doing it."[11] While Porter had worn outrageous costumes (including skirts) on the red carpet before, his hybrid male-female outfit with its enormous hooped skirt was an in-your-face fashion statement, calculated to turn heads at the entertainment world's biggest event. Yet the classic styling was also a respectful nod to fashion and Hollywood history.

In December 2020, singer-actor Harry Styles appeared on the cover of *Vogue* wearing a black tuxedo jacket and gray smocked lace evening gown, both by Gucci. The jacket came from the menswear collection and the gown from the womenswear collection; tellingly, though, *Vogue* simply identified both as "Gucci." There is no more menswear or womenswear, it implied; there is only fashion. The cover—released during a global pandemic—sparked debate about the meaning of masculinity on social media and provoked outrage among conservative commentators, which was curious. Not only did Styles have a long history of embracing gender-bending fashion— wearing pearls and Peter Pan collars, sheer chiffon, pastels and polka dots, feather boas and fur coats—but the gown's long, ruffled skirt was barely visible in the cover image. At a glance, it was not immediately evident that he was wearing a dress, as it had been with Cobain on the cover of *The Face*. But unlike

The Face, Vogue is a women's fashion magazine—*the* women's fashion magazine—and Styles was the first solo man to grace its cover. The inside images—also widely circulated on social media—showed him at full length in the gown, as well as in kilts and a crinoline and pink tulle skirt worn over wide-legged pants. Some of the garments he modeled were designed for men and fell within the bounds of traditional menswear, like a Comme des Garçons Homme Plus kilt; other were women's garments appropriated by a long-haired, baby-faced young man.

Two days after rapper Lil Nas X accidentally split his pants while performing on *Saturday Night Live* in 2021, he appeared on *The Tonight Show* wearing a skirt. The red tartan pattern and box pleats bore a passing resemblance to a kilt, but, unlike a traditional kilt, it fell below the knee, and it wasn't wrapped and fastened at one side. It was clearly not a masculine kilt but a "menswear skirt," as *GQ* dubbed it, paired with an ivory blazer, a bare chest, and black combat boots. Lil Nas X himself called it a skirt: "Stop asking me why I'm wearing a skirt," he tweeted, after posting photos of the prerecorded interview online. "I will never trust pants again!" *GQ* called his "grunge-casual" look—from Virgil Abloh's menswear collection for Louis Vuitton—"the latest sign that the skirt, or dress, is evolving into a standard garment in American menswear."[12]

It's too early to say definitively whether this creative and individualistic blending of masculine and feminine garments, accessories, and cosmetics is a passing fad or a new "standard," either in fashion or in gender expression. But men in skirts will remain shocking as long as they are still considered exclusively "female" garments; in that sense, the current controversy over men in skirts is analogous to the one that greeted women wearing pants and may be just as transitory. Women never stopped wearing dresses, and it is likely that men will continue wearing pants even as skirts become normalized. But it's a barrier broken—a Pandora's dressing-up box that won't be closed again. The future of skirts? It might just be male.

BIBLIOGRAPHY

Abramsky, Sasha. *Little Wonder: The Fabulous Story of Lottie Dod, the World's First Female Sports Superstar.* New York: Akashic Books, 2020.

Alsop, Susan Mary. *To Marietta from Paris, 1945–1960.* New York: Doubleday, 1975.

Anderson, Ann. *High School Prom: Marketing, Morals and the American Teen.* Jefferson, NC: McFarland & Co., 2012.

Antonelli, Paola, et al. *Items: Is Fashion Modern?* New York: The Museum of Modern Art, 2017.

Baker, Carroll. *Baby Doll: An Autobiography.* New York: Arbor House, 1983.

Ballard, Bettina. *In My Fashion.* London: V&A Publishing, 2017.

Barber, Elizabeth Wayland. *Women's Work: The First 20,000 Years; Women, Cloth, and Society in Early Times.* New York: W. W. Norton, 1994.

Bass-Krueger, Maude, and Sophie Kurkdjian, eds. *French Fashion, Women, and the First World War.* New York: Bard Graduate Center, 2019.

Benbow-Pfalzgraf, Taryn, and Richard Martin, eds. *Contemporary Fashion.* New York: St. James Press, 2002.

Bender, Marylin. *The Beautiful People.* New York: Coward-McCann, 1967.

Best, Amy L. *Prom Night: Youth, Schools and Popular Culture.* New York: Routledge, 2000.

Birnbach, Lisa, et al. *The Official Preppy Handbook.* New York: Workman Publishing, 1980.

Black, Prudence, and Stephen Muecke. "The Power of a Dress: the Rhetoric of a Moment in Fashion." In *Rebirth of Rhetoric: Essays in Language, Culture and Education,* edited by Richard Andrews, 212–27. London: Routledge, 1992.

Blakesley, Katie Clark. "'A Style of Our Own': Modesty and Mormon Women, 1951–2008." *Dialogue: A Journal of Mormon Thought* 42, no. 2 (Summer 2009): 20–53.

Blume, Mary. *The Master of Us All: Balenciaga, His Workrooms, His World.* New York: Farrar, Straus and Giroux, 2014.

Bolton, Andrew. *Bravehearts: Men in Skirts.* London: Victoria & Albert Museum, 2003.

Bradley, Barry W. *Galanos.* Cleveland: Western Reserve Historical Society, 1996.

Brownie, Barbara. *Spacewear: Weightlessness and the Final Frontier of Fashion.* London: Bloomsbury Visual Arts, 2019.

Carter, Ernestine. *With Tongue in Chic.* London: V&A Publishing, 2020.

Chamberlain, Lindy. *Through My Eyes: An Autobiography.* Melbourne: William Heinemann Australia, 1990.

Chrisman-Campbell, Kimberly. "*Cinderella:* The Ultimate (Postwar) Makeover Story." *The Atlantic,* March 2015. https://www.theatlantic.com/entertainment/archive/2015/03/cinderella-the-ultimate-postwar-makeover-story/387229/.

Chrisman-Campbell, Kimberly. "The Midi Skirt, Divider of Nations." *The Atlantic,* September 2014. https://www.theatlantic.com/entertainment/archive/2014/09/the-return-of-the-midi-skirt/379543/.

Chrisman-Campbell, Kimberly. "When American Suffragists Tried to 'Wear the Pants.'" *The Atlantic,* June 2019. https://www.theatlantic.com/entertainment/archive/2019/06/merican-suffragists-bloomers-pants-history/591484/#:~:text=Women%20demanded%20physical%20freedom%20along,%2C%20in%20other%20words%2C%20pants.

Chrisman-Campbell, Kimberly. "Wimbledon's First Fashion Scandal." *The Atlantic,* July 2019. https://www.theatlantic.com/entertainment/archive/2019/07/suzanne-leglen-wimbledon-fashion-scandal-tennis/593443/.

Coleman, Elizabeth Ann. *The Genius of Charles James.* New York: Henry Holt & Co., 1984.

Cooper, Lady Diana. *The Rainbow Comes and Goes.* New York: Vintage Digital, 2018.

Cosgrave, Bronwyn. *Made for Each Other: Fashion and the Academy Awards.* London: Bloomsbury, 2007.

Cullen, Oriole, and Sonnet Stanfill. *Ballgowns: British Glamour Since 1950*. London: Victoria & Albert Museum, 2013.

Danzig, Allison, and Peter Schwed, eds. *The Fireside Book of Tennis*. New York: Simon & Schuster, 1972.

Deihl, Nancy, ed. *The Hidden History of American Fashion: Rediscovering 20th-Century Women Designers*. New York: Bloomsbury Academic, 2018.

Diliberto, Gioia. *Diane von Furstenberg: A Life Unwrapped*. New York: HarperCollins, 2015.

Dior, Christian. *Christian Dior and I*. New York: Dutton, 1957.

Dior, Christian. *Dior by Dior: The Autobiography of Christian Dior*. London: V&A Publishing, 2018.

Farrell-Beck, Jane, and Colleen Gau. *Uplift: The Bra in America*. Philadelphia: University of Pennsylvania Press, 2002.

Ford, Henry, with Samuel Crowther. *My Life and Work*. Garden City, NY: Doubleday, Page & Co., 1922.

Ford, Richard Thompson. *Dress Codes: How the Laws of Fashion Made History*. New York: Simon & Schuster, 2021.

Francke, Linda Bird. "Princess of Fashion." *Newsweek*, March 22, 1976, 52–58.

Fraser, Kennedy. *The Fashionable Mind*. Boston, MA: Nonpareil Books, 1985.

Harvey, John. *The Story of Black*. London: Reaktion Books, 2015.

Head, Edith, and Paddy Calistro McAuley. *Edith Head's Hollywood*. New York: Dutton, 1983.

Head, Edith. *The Dress Doctor: Prescriptions for Style, from A to Z*. New York: Harper Design, 2011.

Hill, Colleen. *Reinvention and Restlessness: Fashion in the Nineties*. New York: Rizzoli Electa, 2021.

Hollander, Anne. *Seeing Through Clothes*. Berkeley: University of California Press, 1993.

Howell, Georgina. *Sultans of Style: Thirty Years of Fashion and Passion, 1960–1990*. London: Ebury Press, 1990.

Hulanicki, Barbara. *From A to Biba: The Autobiography of Barbara Hulanicki*. London: V&A Publishing, 2018.

Ironside, Janey. *Janey: An Autobiography*. London: V&A Publishing, 1990.

Jones, Kevin, and Christina Johnson. *Sporting Fashion: Outdoor Girls 1800 to 1960*. New York: Prestel and American Federation of Arts, 2021.

Jorgensen, Jay. *Edith Head: The Fifty-Year Career of Hollywood's Greatest Costume Designer.* Philadelphia, PA: Running Press, 2010.

Koda, Harold, and Andrew Bolton. *Schiaparelli & Prada: Impossible Conversations.* New York: Metropolitan Museum of Art, 2012.

Koda, Harold, Jan Glier Reeder, et al. *Charles James: Beyond Fashion.* New York: Metropolitan Museum of Art, 2014.

Koda, Harold. *Goddess: The Classical Mode.* New York: Metropolitan Museum of Art, 2003.

Lethbridge, Lucy. *Servants: A Downstairs History of Britain from the Nineteenth Century to Modern Times.* New York: W. W. Norton, 2013.

Levin, Diane E., and Jean Kilbourne. *So Sexy So Soon: The New Sexualized Childhood, and What Parents Can Do to Protect Their Kids.* New York: Ballantine Books, 2008.

Lichtman, Sarah. "'Teenagers Have Taken over the House': Print Marketing, Teenage Girls, and the Representation, Decoration, and Design of the Postwar Home, c. 1945–1965." PhD diss., Bard Graduate Center for Studies in the Decorative Arts, Design, and Culture, 2013.

Loriot, Thierry-Maxime, ed. *The Fashion World of Jean Paul Gaultier: From the Sidewalk to the Catwalk.* Montreal: Montreal Museum of Fine Arts and Abrams Books, 2011.

Lynam, Ruth, ed. *Couture: An Illustrated History of the Great Paris Designers and Their Creations.* Garden City, NY: Doubleday, 1972.

Martin, Mary. *My Heart Belongs.* New York: William Morrow, 1976.

Martin, Richard. *American Ingenuity: Sportswear, 1930s–1970s.* New York: Metropolitan Museum of Art, 1998.

Miller, Daniel, and Sophie Woodward. *Blue Jeans: The Art of the Ordinary.* Berkeley: University of California Press, 2012.

Mirabella, Grace, with Judith Warner. *In and Out of Vogue: A Memoir.* New York: Doubleday, 1995.

Mitford, Nancy, and Charlotte Mosley, ed. *Love from Nancy: The Letters of Nancy Mitford.* New York: Houghton Mifflin Harcourt, 1993.

Molloy, John T. *New Women's Dress for Success.* New York: Grand Central Publishing, 2008.

Molloy, John T. *The Woman's Dress for Success Book.* New York: Follett Publishing, 1977.

Mower, Sarah, and Anna Wintour. *Oscar: The Style, Inspiration and Life of Oscar de la Renta.* New York: Assouline, 2002.

Mulvagh, Jane. *Vogue History of 20th Century Fashion*. New York: Viking, 1989.

Nichols, Nichelle. *Beyond Uhura: Star Trek and Other Memories*. New York: G. P. Putnam's, 1994.

Paulicelli, Eugenia. *Italian Style: Fashion & Film from Early Cinema to the Digital Age*. London: Bloomsbury Academic, 2016.

Perkins, Jeanne. "Dior," *LIFE*, March 1, 1948.

Picardie, Justine. *Miss Dior*. New York: Farrar, Straus and Giroux, 2021.

Poiret, Paul. *King of Fashion: The Autobiography of Paul Poiret*. London: V&A Publishing, 2019.

Quant, Mary. *Mary Quant: Autobiography*. London: Headline Publishing Group, 2012.

Quant, Mary. *Quant by Quant: The Autobiography of Mary Quant*. London: V&A Publishing, 2018.

Ribeiro, Aileen. *Dress and Morality*. London: Batsford, 1986.

Richardson, Kristen. *The Season: A Social History of the Debutante*. New York: W. W. Norton, 2020.

Schiaparelli, Elsa. *Shocking Life*. New York: Dutton, 1954.

Snow, Carmel, with Mary Louise Aswell. *The World of Carmel Snow*. London: V&A Publishing, 2017.

Steele, Valerie. *Women of Fashion: Twentieth Century Designers*. New York: Rizzoli, 1991.

Streisand, Barbra. *My Passion for Design*. New York: Viking, 2010.

Stuart, Amanda Mackenzie. *Empress of Fashion: A Life of Diana Vreeland*. New York: Harper, 2012.

Sutherland, Christine. *Marie Walewska: Napoleon's Great Love*. New York: Robin Clark, 1986.

Syme, Rachel. "The Allure of the Nap Dress, the Look of Gussied-Up Oblivion." *The New Yorker*, July 21, 2020. https://www.newyorker.com/culture/on-and-off-the-avenue/the-allure-of-the-nap-dress-the-look-of-gussied-up-oblivion.

Von Furstenberg, Diane, with Linda Bird Francke. *Diane: A Signature Life*. New York: Simon & Schuster, 1998.

Von Furstenberg, Diane. *The Woman I Wanted to Be*. New York: Simon & Schuster, 2014.

Webb, Iain R. *Foale and Tuffin: The Sixties; A Decade in Fashion*. London: ACC Publishing Group, 2009.

White, Palmer. *Poiret*. New York: Clarkson N. Potter, 1973.

Whitmore, Lucie. "'A Matter of Individual Opinion and Feeling': The Changing Culture of Mourning Dress in the First World War." *Women's History Review* 27, no. 4 (2018): 579–94.

Wilson, Elizabeth. *Love Game: A History of Tennis, from Victorian Pastime to Global Phenomenon*. Chicago: University of Chicago Press, 2016.

Yoxall, H. W. *A Fashion of Life*. London: William Heinemann, 1966.

NOTES

INTRODUCTION

1. Elizabeth Wayland Barber, *Women's Work: The First 20,000 Years; Women, Cloth, and Society in Early Times* (New York: W. W. Norton, 1995), 59.

2. Harold Koda and Andrew Bolton, *Schiaparelli & Prada: Impossible Conversations* (New York: Metropolitan Museum of Art, 2012), 174.

3. Valerie Steele, interviewed in Thierry-Maxime Loriot, ed., *The Fashion World of Jean Paul Gaultier: From the Sidewalk to the Catwalk* (Montreal: Montreal Museum of Fine Arts and Abrams Books, 2011), 152.

4. "Girl in Pants Goes to Court," *The Journal Times,* January 9, 1943.

5. Yanan Wang, "Pennsylvania Girl Says She Was Thrown out of Her Prom for Wearing a Suit," *The Washington Post,* May 9, 2016.

1. THE DELPHOS

1. Palmer White, *Poiret* (New York: Clarkson N. Potter, 1973), 29.

2. Lady Diana Cooper, *The Rainbow Comes and Goes* (New York: Vintage Digital, 2018), 44.

3. Harold Koda, *Goddess: The Classical Mode* (New York: Metropolitan Museum of Art, 2003), 18.

4. Quoted in Christine Sutherland, *Marie Walewska: Napoleon's Great Love* (New York: Robin Clark, 1986), 111.

5. Cooper, *The Rainbow Comes and Goes,* 44.

6. "The Prophet of Simplicity," *Vogue,* November 1, 1913; "Poiret on the Philosophy of Dress," *Vogue,* October 15, 1913.

7. Cooper, *The Rainbow Comes and Goes,* 44.

8. H. W. Yoxall, *A Fashion of Life* (London: William Heinemann, 1966), 102, 49.

9. Madeleine Ginsburg, "The Thirties: Artistry and Fantasy," in *Couture: An Illustrated History of the Great Paris Designers and Their Creations,* ed. Ruth Lynam (Garden City, NY: Doubleday, 1972), 105, 91–112.

10. Penelope Portrait, "A Paris Model: The World of Mannequins," in Lynam, *Couture,* 186, 178–191.

11. Bettina Ballard, *In My Fashion* (London: V&A Publishing, 2017), 19.

12. One of Martin's costumes, a beaded peach georgette "Grecian" gown and matching stole, survives in the Museum of the City of New York (acc. no. 68.128.13A-C); "Mainbocher Honored at N.Y. Benefit," *The Globe and Mail,* January 24, 1984.

13. FIDM Museum and Galleries, acc. no. 77.1948.008.16.

14. Megan Mellbye, *Galanos on Galanos* (Princeton, NJ: Films for the Humanities & Sciences, 2003). Examples from the collection survive in The Museum at FIT (acc. no. 86.80.1) and the Metropolitan Museum of Art (acc. nos. 1970.279.10 and 2009.300.7966a–d).

2. THE TENNIS SKIRT

1. Elizabeth Wilson, *Love Game: A History of Tennis, from Victorian Pastime to Global Phenomenon* (Chicago: University of Chicago Press, 2016), 33.

2. Letter to Arnold Herschell, quoted in Sasha Abramsky, *Little Wonder: The Fabulous Story of Lottie Dod, the World's First Female Sports Superstar* (New York: Akashic Books, 2020), 187.

3. Jeane Hoffman, "The Sutton Sisters," in Allison Danzig and Peter Schwed, eds., *The Fireside Book of Tennis* (New York: Simon & Schuster, 1972), 74.

4. Ted Tinling, "Fashion's Serve: Dressed to Win," *The New York Times,* June 19, 1977.

3. THE LITTLE BLACK DRESS

1. John Harvey, *The Story of Black* (London: Reaktion Books, 2015), 264.

2. "Introducing the Most Chic Woman in the World," *Vogue,* January 1, 1926.

3. Lucy Lethbridge, *Servants: A Downstairs History of Britain from the Nineteenth Century to Modern Times* (New York: W. W. Norton, 2013), 44.

4. Maude Bass-Krueger, "Mourning," in *French Fashion, Women, and the First World War,* eds. Maude Bass-Kreuger and Sophie Kurkdjian (New York: Bard Graduate Center, 2019), 203.

5. Lucie Whitmore, "'A Matter of Individual Opinion and Feeling': The Changing Culture of Mourning Dress in the First World War," *Women's History Review* 27, no. 4 (2018): 585–86.

6. "Woman's Place Is in a Uniform," *Vogue,* July 1, 1918, 35; A.S., "Paris Lifts Ever so Little the Ban on Gaiety," *Vogue,* November 15, 1916, 43.

7. Quoted in Jane Mulvagh, *Vogue History of 20th Century Fashion* (New York: Viking, 1989), 49.

8. "Substitutes for the Strict Tailleur," *Vogue,* March 15, 1924, 58.

9. Carmel Snow with Mary Louise Aswell, *The World of Carmel Snow* (London: V&A Publishing, 2017), 29.

10. Ballard, *In My Fashion,* 55.

11. Yoxall, *A Fashion of Life,* 60.

12. Mary Quant, *Mary Quant: Autobiography* (London: Headline Publishing Group, 2012), 162.

13. Daniel Miller and Sophie Woodward, *Blue Jeans: The Art of the Ordinary* (Berkeley: University of California Press, 2012), 78–83.

14. Quoted in Marie-Andrée Jouve and Jacqueline Demornex, *Balenciaga* (London: Thames & Hudson, 1989), 96.

15. Hal Rubenstein, *100 Unforgettable Dresses* (New York: HarperDesign, 2011), 17.

16. Ernestine Carter, *With Tongue in Chic* (London: V&A Publishing, 2020).

4. THE WRAP DRESS

1. See, for example, Eleanor Page, "Charles James' Initial Designs Led to Scandal," *Chicago Tribune,* November 12, 1974.

2. Elizabeth Ann Coleman, *The Genius of Charles James* (New York: Henry Holt & Co., 1984), 111.

3. Coleman, *The Genius of Charles James,* 86, n. 30.

4. Coleman, *The Genius of Charles James*, 109.

5. John Duka, "The Ghost of Seventh Avenue," *New York*, October 16, 1978, 91.

6. Blanche Grace Davis, "Youthful Designer McCardell Creates for Very Young," *Knoxville News-Sentinel*, August 1, 1944.

7. Diane von Furstenberg with Linda Bird Francke, *Diane: A Signature Life* (New York: Simon & Schuster, 1998), 80–81, 74.

8. Margaria Fichtner, "The Designer Who Put Dresses Back on Women," *Miami Herald*, October 19, 1976.

9. Gioia Diliberto, *Diane von Furstenberg: A Life Unwrapped* (New York: HarperCollins, 2015), 111.

10. Linda Bird Francke, "Princess of Fashion," *Newsweek*, March 22, 1976, 58, 55.

11. Gioia Diliberto, *Diane von Furstenberg: A Life Unwrapped* (New York: HarperCollins, 2015), 147.

12. Jerry Bowles, "Diane Von Furstenberg—at the Top," *Vogue*, July 1, 1976, 141.

13. Diliberto, *Diane von Furstenberg*, 109.

14. Carola Long, "Wrap Superstar," *The Independent EXTRA*, March 27, 2008, 4.

15. Diliberto, *Diane von Furstenberg*, 109.

16. Diliberto, *Diane von Furstenberg*, 109, 146–47.

17. "Is Fashion Working for Women? A Vogue Symposium," *Vogue*, January 1985, 204–8, 274–75.

5. THE STRAPLESS DRESS

1. Quoted in Aileen Ribeiro, *Dress and Morality* (London: Batsford, 1986), 159.

2. Alicia Hart, "Shoulders Must Have Beauty in Strapless Gown," *Spokane Chronicle*, September 8, 1938.

3. "Consider the Basis of Your Spring Suit," *The Montclair Times*, March 27, 1936.

4. Helen Fraser, "'Whoops, My Dear'—Watch Your Wide Crinoline Skirts," *The Province*, November 12, 1938.

5. Brenda Frazier, "My Debut—A Horror," *LIFE*, December 6, 1963, 141.

6. Monique, "Latest from Paris," *Daily News,* May 31, 1952.

7. "Princess Margaret Selects Strapless Dancing Frock," *The Calgary Herald,* November 18, 1949.

8. Harold Koda, Jan Glier Reeder, et al. *Charles James: Beyond Fashion* (New York: Metropolitan Museum of Art, 2014), 30.

9. Coleman, *The Genius of Charles James,* 107.

10. Edith Head, *Edith Head's Hollywood* (New York: Dutton, 1983), 96.

11. "Chicago Debutante Cotillion," *Vogue,* December 1, 1949, 93; Eleanor Page, "Gown to Be Reward for Debutante," *Chicago Tribune,* August 17, 1949.

12. Kristen Richardson, *The Season: A Social History of the Debutante* (New York: W. W. Norton, 2020), 168.

13. Janey Ironside, *Janey: An Autobiography* (London: V&A Publishing, 1990), 82.

14. Richard Gehman, "The Nine Billion Dollars in Hot Little Hands," *Cosmopolitan,* November 1957, 72–79.

15. Ann Anderson, *High School Prom: Marketing, Morals and the American Teen* (Jefferson, NC: McFarland & Co., 2012), 7.

16. "Teen-agers to Get Chic New Fashions," *The New York Times,* August 27, 1946.

17. Katie Clark Blakesley, "'A Style of Our Own': Modesty and Mormon Women, 1951–2008," *Dialogue: A Journal of Mormon Thought* 42, no. 2 (Summer 2009): 22.

18. Sarah Lichtman, "'Teenagers Have Taken over the House': Print Marketing, Teenage Girls, and the Representation, Decoration, and Design of the Postwar Home, c. 1945–1965" (PhD diss., Bard Graduate Center for Studies in the Decorative Arts, Design, and Culture, 2013), 263.

19. "Two Good Reasons," *The Cincinnati Enquirer,* December 4, 1953.

20. Marylin Bender, "Strapless Dress of the 40's Takes On New Airs for '65," *The New York Times,* August 11, 1965.

21. Sergio Bichao, "Readington Board Revises Strapless-dress Ban," *The Central New Jersey Home News,* May 3, 2013.

22. Richard Thompson Ford, *Dress Codes: How the Laws of Fashion Made History* (New York: Simon & Schuster, 2021), 239, 242, 245, 246.

6. THE BAR SUIT

1. Christian Dior, *Dior by Dior: The Autobiography of Christian Dior* (London: V&A Publishing, 2018), 25–26.

2. Ballard, *In My Fashion*, 244.

3. Ernestine Carter, *With Tongue in Chic* (London: V&A Publishing, 2020), 72.

4. Dior, *Dior by Dior*, 20.

5. Carter, *With Tongue in Chic*, 72.

6. Ballard, *In My Fashion*, 245.

7. Susan Mary Alsop, *To Marietta from Paris, 1945–1960* (New York: Doubleday, 1975), 93.

8. Carter, *With Tongue in Chic*, 72.

9. Dior, *Dior by Dior*, 27.

10. Carter, *With Tongue in Chic*, 73.

11. Ballard, *In My Fashion*, 245.

12. Carter, *With Tongue in Chic*, 73.

13. Dior, *Dior by Dior*, 29, 24.

14. Christian Dior, *Christian Dior and I* (New York: Dutton, 1957), 40.

15. Dior, *Dior by Dior*, 138.

16. Jeanne Perkins, "Dior," *LIFE*, March 1, 1948, 90.

17. Justine Picardie, *Miss Dior* (New York: Farrar, Straus and Giroux, 2021), 324.

18. Dior, *Dior by Dior*, 170.

7. THE NAKED DRESS

1. Herb Stein, "Best of Hollywood," *The Philadelphia Inquirer*, February 4, 1958.

2. Bronwyn Cosgrave, *Made for Each Other: Fashion and the Academy Awards* (London: Bloomsbury, 2007).

3. "Fashion Comes from What the Young Wear," *The Baltimore Sun*, February 2, 1969.

4. Colleen Hill, *Reinvention and Restlessness: Fashion in the Nineties* (New York: Rizzoli Electa, 2021), 20.

5. Eric Schmidt, "The Tinkerer's Apprentice," Project Syndicate, January 19, 2015, https://www.project-syndicate.org/onpoint/google

-european-commission-and-disruptive-technological-change-by-eric
-schmidt-2015-01.

6. Robin Givhan, "Jennifer Lopez's Fashion Blunder at Ameri-can Music Awards," *The Daily Beast,* November 21, 2011, https://www.thedailybeast.com/jennifer-lopezs-fashion-blunder-at-american-music-awards.

8. THE MINISKIRT

1. Quant, *Mary Quant,* 275.

2. Iain R. Webb, *Foale and Tuffin: The Sixties; A Decade in Fashion* (London: ACC Publishing Group, 2009), 110.

3. Barbara Hulanicki, *From A to Biba: The Autobiography of Barbara Hulanicki* (London: V&A Publishing, 2018), 62, 58, 64.

4. Carter, *With Tongue in Chic,* 142.

5. "The Lord of the Space Ladies," *LIFE,* May 21, 1965, 47; Carter, *With Tongue in Chic,* 169.

6. Marylin Bender, *The Beautiful People* (New York: Coward-McCann, 1967), 55.

7. Barbara Brownie, *Spacewear: Weightlessness and the Final Frontier of Fashion* (London: Bloomsbury Visual Arts, 2019), 11, 25.

8. Nichelle Nichols, *Beyond Uhura: Star Trek and Other Memories* (New York: G. P. Putnam's, 1994), 169.

9. Quoted in Ann Ryan and Serena Sinclair, "Space Age Fashion," in Lynam, *Couture,* 198, 192–222.

10. Carter, *With Tongue in Chic,* 162.

11. Mary Blume, *The Master of Us All: Balenciaga, His Workrooms, His World* (New York: Farrar, Straus and Giroux, 2014), 171.

12. Webb, *Foale and Tuffin,* 148.

13. Quoted in Mulvagh, *Vogue History of 20th Century Fashion,* 239.

14. Webb, *Foale and Tuffin,* 152.

15. Bender, *The Beautiful People,* 234.

16. Prudence Black and Stephen Muecke, "The Power of a Dress: The Rhetoric of a Moment in Fashion," in *Rebirth of Rhetoric: Essays in Language, Culture and Education,* ed. Richard Andrews (London: Routledge, 1992), 218.

17. "Knee Line," *The English Digest* 57 (1958): 48.

18. Portrait, "A Paris Model," 187.

9. THE MIDI SKIRT

1. Marylin Bedner, "The Girls in Their Summer Dresses: Keeping the Miniskirt Alive," *The New York Times*, July 5, 1968.

2. Marylou Luther, "Is Europe Fashion Domination Ending?" *Los Angeles Times*, May 20, 1973; Kennedy Fraser, *The Fashionable Mind* (Boston, MA: Nonpareil Books, 1985), 3.

3. "The Midi's Compensations," *Time*, June 8, 1970, 50; "Hold That Mini Line!" *Time*, August 8, 1969, 60; Bernadine Morris, "Hemlines: A Matter of Choice," *The New York Times*, July 3, 1984.

4. "Fashion Fascism: The Politics of Midi," *Rags*, October 1970.

5. "The Midi Muscles In," *LIFE*, August 21, 1970, 22–29.

6. Carrie Donovan, "Short-Circuiting the Short Skirt," *The New York Times*, April 25, 1982.

7. Sharon Barrett, "Shoppers Sharper; Fads Fade Faster," *Pittsburgh Post-Gazette*, April 2, 1983.

8. Quoted in Kristen Bateman, "Why Cottagecore and Prairie Dressing Are Fashion's Biggest Trends in 2020," *Teen Vogue*, May 8, 2020.

10. THE BODYCON DRESS

1. Jay Jorgensen, *Edith Head: The Fifty-Year Career of Hollywood's Greatest Costume Designer* (Philadelphia, PA: Running Press, 2010), 42.

2. "Hobble Skirt Furnishes Newest Railroad Danger," *The Sun*, September 7, 1913.

3. "Plunging Neckline, Falsies Get Blame for Rise in Sex Crimes," *Brooklyn Eagle*, December 16, 1949.

4. Bernadine Morris, "Strapless 40's Return in Style to Suit the 70's," *The New York Times*, February 21, 1973.

5. Georgina Howell, *Sultans of Style: Thirty Years of Fashion and Passion, 1960–1990* (London: Ebury Press, 1990), 158.

6. Marylou Luther, "Design Maverick Azzedine Alaia Sculpts His One-of-a-KindNiche," *Los Angeles Times*, July 6, 1984.

7. Fraser, *Fashionable Mind*, 232–33.

8. Jill Gerston, "Caution: Curves Ahead," *Austin American-Statesman*, August 13, 1986.

9. Gerston, "Caution: Curves Ahead."

10. Howell, *Sultans of Style*, 161–62.

11. Julie Hatfield, "Squabbling in Style," *The Boston Globe*, January 8, 1987.

12. Susie Rushton, "Close Encounters," *The Independent* (London) Magazine, June 30, 2007, 42.

13. Leah Melby Clinton, "The History of the Bandage Dress, From 1994 to Now," *Glamour*, September 23, 2015, https://www.glamour.com /story/history-herve-leger-bandage-dress.

14. Quoted in Amanda Mackenzie Stuart, *Empress of Fashion: A Life of Diana Vreeland* (New York: Harper, 2012), 250.

15. Alexandra Jacobs, "Smooth Moves: How Sara Blakely Rehabilitated the Girdle," *The New Yorker*, March 28, 2011.

16. Maureen Sajbel, "Tightly Wound: Herve Leger's Bandage-Wrap Dresses Appeal to Those Who Dare to Bare," *Los Angeles Times*, December 8, 1994.

CONCLUSION

1. James B. Stewart, "A Genius of the Storefront, Too," *The New York Times*, October 16, 2011.

2. Joanne McNeil, "The End of Sexism," Mediaite, September 25, 2010, https://www.mediaite.com/online/the-end-of-sexism/.

3. Andrew Sadauskas, "'What You Can't Measure You Can't Manage': Empathy the Key to More Diversity in Tech," SmartCompany, December 9, 2014, https://www.smartcompany.com.au/startupsmart /advice/leadership-advice/qwhat-you-cant-measure-you-cant -manageq-empathy-the-key-to-more-diversity-in-tech/.

4. Nichole Sullivan, "Sexist by Design?" *Stubbornella*, May 9, 2014, http://www.stubbornella.org/content/.

5. Carolina A. Miranda, "Wanted: Male Architect Willing to Navigate His Own Building in a Skirt," *Los Angeles Times*, July 15, 2018, https://www.latimes.com/entertainment/arts/miranda/la-et-cam -male-design-in-architecture-20180714-story.html; "Women Warned About Glass Staircase at New Courthouse," 10tv.com, June 11, 2001, https://www.10tv.com/article/news/women-warned-about-glass -staircase-new-courthouse/530-d9089684-3854-458f-b9a7-6379b8888bc4.

6. Anne Hollander, *Seeing Through Clothes* (Berkeley: University of California Press, 1993), 218.

7. Quoted in Ford, *Dress Codes*, 258.

8. "You Can Thank Stacey Plaskett's College Friends For Her Viral Blue Impeachment Dress," *Elle*, March 17, 2021, https://www.elle.com /culture/career-politics/a35743131/stacey-plaskett-impeachment-trial -blue-dress/.

9. Amanda Platell, "How Margaret Thatcher Taught Me Powerful Women Never Wear Trousers," *Daily Mail Online*, November 4, 2015.

10. Andrew Bolton, *Bravehearts: Men in Skirts* (London: Victoria & Albert Museum, 2003), 138.

11. Billy Porter, *Actors on Actors: Billy Porter and Rachel Brosnahan*, Variety Studio, June 2019, https://variety.com/video/actors-on-actors -billy-porter-rachel-brosnahan-full-video/?jwsource=cl.

12. Rachel Tashjian, "Lil Nas X Joins the Great Menswear Skirt Movement," *GQ.com*, May 25, 2021, https://www.gq.com/story/lil-nas-x-plaid -skirt.

INDEX

NOTE: Page numbers in *italics* indicate photographs